Amir M Ismail is an Associate with Holmes Mackillop Limited, solicitors, in Glasgow. Having graduated from the University of Strathclyde with an LLB (Honours) in 2005, he subsequently completed the Diploma in Legal Practice and then started his legal career as a trainee solicitor in August 2006 with HBM Sayers.

Amir always knew he wanted to practice solely in Property Law at a very early stage and he has never worked in any other area of law, having completed his 2 year specialised traineeship in Commercial Property in August 2008. Amir joined Holmes Mackillop in February 2015 and, throughout his working life, he has undertaken a wide variety of commercial property work. He is experienced in all aspects of the sale, purchase and lending aspects of commercial property, including site acquisition, development, plot sales, investment properties, offices, shops and industrial units.

Amir also undertakes a large volume of commercial leasing work, representing the interests of numerous Landlords and Tenants across the whole of Scotland, with a view to securing a commercially viable agreement in each case. Amir has tutored in both Residential Conveyancing and Commercial Conveyancing on the Diploma in Legal Practice course at Glasgow University since October 2014. He thoroughly enjoys working with students and clients alike, as well as fellow practitioners, and is also involved in the delivery of CPD to the legal profession for MBL Seminars Limited, CCPD Training Limited and the Law Society of Scotland.

A Practical Guide to Ending Commercial Leases in Scotland

A Practical Guide to Ending Commercial Leases in Scotland

Amir M Ismail
LLB (Hons), Dip LP
Associate in Commercial Property at Holmes Mackillop
Tutor in Residential and Commercial Conveyancing on the Diploma in Legal Practice at the University of Glasgow

Law Brief Publishing

Published 2021 by Law Brief Publishing, an imprint of Law Brief Publishing Ltd
30 The Parks
Minehead
Somerset
TA24 8BT

www.lawbriefpublishing.com

Paperback: 978-1-913715-30-4

PREFACE AND LIGHT INTRODUCTION

Commercial Property is, in my view, an exciting and varied area of legal practice. It encompasses a fine balance between fundamental legal principles and many aspects of practicality – irrespective of whether acting for a Seller, Purchaser, Landlord or Tenant. For me, personally, working in this area of property law reflects my ongoing approval of the underpinning principles of certainty and protection of the 3rd party over fairness alone. Separately, it introduces a business reality and diversity of workload that is not replicated in any other area of law. All the necessary aspects of the jigsaw puzzle should fit together to form a skilled and seamless service delivered by a commercial property solicitor to a client in modern practice, but it is essential that any practitioner has a firm grasp and understanding of the main aspects and ancillary areas. This will ensure that the risk of a claim for professional negligence is minimised (if not eradicated altogether).

For many years I have worked with practitioners and students alike, who have expressed a desire for someone to put together a short, but succinct, manual on the essential aspects to consider when terminating a commercial Lease in Scotland. The present position is not neatly packaged in one place and, in my view, consists of a fine mix of statutes and common law cases. It will no doubt continue to develop and evolve further with the passage of time. The global pandemic known as Coronavirus created a set of circumstances early in 2020 where everything that I once enjoyed was no longer an option. As such, and with my usual routine severely disrupted, that "*someone*" unexpectedly turned out to be myself!

I know only too well that the modern practitioner does not always have the time or resources to research specific aspects of law and/or practice. I hope that this book will be of equal benefit to experienced practitioners looking to firm up their "*gut feeling*" just as much as students and trainees that are starting out in their journey into the world of commercial leasing. The law is stated to be accurate, as at 1st December 2020, and there is a separate chapter analysing and commenting on present proposals for reform at the end.

There are a number of people that will forever receive my gratitude in completing this book. A massive thanks must go to Tim Kevan and Garry Wright at Law Brief Publishing, whose persistency and support throughout was pivotal in getting this book "*on the shelf*". Similarly, my family – I don't think any child will ever repay their parents properly for all the time, effort and guidance they give whilst we have them in our lives – and mine are no exception to this. My work colleagues, past and present, including Bill Duffy and Kevin Thompson, were instrumental in my decision to pull this all together, and their patience and understanding in giving me sufficient time to write these presents will not be forgotten. It goes without saying many of my clients would rather I continued to "*fight their corner*" instead of taking a few days off to write a book, but we managed to juggle competing interests so that everyone, including myself, was left happy in the end. The book also brought its own moments of humour too, including Kevin telling me that "*the book will be good for you, and I think you'll be a good author, but you have missed your true calling in life – as a procurator fiscal you would have had most of Scotland in prison by now*"! As much as I don't regret the path I find myself on, I have to say I think I would struggle to accept those of a guilty mindset escaping justice on a technicality – it would ruin too many of my working days to make it all worthwhile! Maybe one day! I also relay my thanks to the team of tutors and staff at the Diploma in Legal Practice at Glasgow University, who, in trusting me with their students every year, gave me the opportunity to see how both the students just as much as myself can improve professionally and personally. Helping the next generation of practitioners remains a large part of my drive and determination to this day.

I would like to dedicate this book to those that have lost loved ones in very difficult, unexpected, and trying circumstances. The strength of their character, resolve, determination and willingness to carry on and start afresh will forever remain in my mind. It is not something that can be taught or prevented, given these things are nothing but a sheer "*luck of the draw*". Their endeavours in moving forward with their lives will be the best way of remembering those that are no longer with us and making them proud of what we will all leave behind one day. As such, I will be donating all proceeds of sale properly payable to me, as author of this book, to the Moira Fund (www.themoirafund.org.uk). This charity works tirelessly to assist those families suffering from bereavement in the most tragic set of circumstances. If you are considering a donation to charity, however small or insignificant, or indeed wish to show any level of appreciation for this book, then I would welcome you considering a donation of any amount to add to my own ongoing donation(s). Separately, any feedback or suggestions for improvement would equally be welcome, by email, to aismail@homack.co.uk.

With sincere thanks and best wishes,

Amir M Ismail
1st December 2020

CONTENTS

CHAPTER ONE

CREATION OF LEASE OBLIGATIONS

A lease, at its very basic level, is a contract between the heritable proprietor of land and a third party, regulating the use and possession of a property, subject to certain conditions. It would make sense, in my mind, to set out the essential requirements for a Lease to be constituted in the first place. It goes without saying that if there is no Lease in existence from day one then there is no contract capable of termination, and the question then becomes one about the recovery of possession from the occupier, through voluntary agreement or judicial intervention.

A lease can be created at common law without it being in writing if it is less than or equal to a year in its duration, failing which, in all other instances, a Lease must be in writing[1].

There are four essential elements required in order to constitute a Lease, at common law or otherwise, and these can be summarised as follows:

(a) Parties

A lease, being a contract between a Landlord and Tenant, requires at least 2 distinct legal entities. The parties in question can be individuals, partnerships, Limited Liability Partnerships, Companies, Trusts, and so forth, but the same party cannot be both Landlord and Tenant in a Lease. There is a stand-alone chapter on *confusio* in this book, so

[1] Sections 1(2)a and 1(7) of the Requirements of Writing (Scotland) Act 1995;

it won't be discussed here, albeit there will be a cross-reference to this section in some instances. In the case of *Kildrummy Estates (Jersey) Limited V Commissioners of Inland Revenue*[2] Lord President Hope emphasised in his judgement that "*the whole basis of a contractual obligation is the agreement of two or more parties as to the act or thing to be done. This is as true of a Lease as it is of any other contract. It is impossible to conceive of a Lease by a man in his own favour......*"[3].

There are 2 cases that go on and emphasise what is and is not permitted under Scots law when parties are not simply different stand-alone entities. *Pinkerton V Pinkerton*[4] involved a Lease being granted by Alexander Pinkerton in favour of his wife, his two sons and himself. The Lease was held to be valid and Lord Mackay of Clashfern commented that "*there is nothing in the authorities...... which would strike at the right of an individual named as one of the tenants to sue to prevent his being denied the character of a co-tenant and thus enforcing the primary obligation on the Landlord to admit him as a co-tenant with others; an attempt on the part of the Landlord to deny him this right would appear to be analogous to a pro indiviso proprietor being subject to encroachment by a co-proprietor.*"[5] This decision, on face value, should work the other way round but this was subsequently held not to be the case. In *Clydesdale Bank Plc V Davidson*[6] it was held that a Lease granted by 3 co-proprietors in favour of 1 co-proprietor was invalid. Lord Clyde commented in his judgement that "*it does not seem to me that any or all of those that are co-proprietors can validly create a lease of the lands in favour of one of their own number. In the present case the appellant was by virtue of his co-ownership entitled to the use of the lands, albeit along with the other co-proprietors. He needed no grant of a right to use or occupy the*

[2] 1991 SC 1

[3] Page 6

[4] 1986 SLT 672

[5] Page 676

[6] 1998 SC (HL) 51

lands. He already had that right. If the others chose to surrender their rights of use so as to leave him in exclusive possession that did not create in him a right of tenancy but simply removed a qualification on the rights which he enjoyed as co-proprietor..... A right of sole occupation cannot co-exist with a right of ownership, albeit co-ownership, in the same person. The greater right must absorb and extinguish the lesser right. The narrow path of which Lord Mackay of Clashfern adopted in Pinkerton V Pinkerton, whereby a Lease could validly be constituted between a sole proprietor and several persons including himself as tenants, is not available where the greater right is held in its entirety by the Landlord."[7] This case should not be seen as conflicting with a Lease by a Partnership in favour of one of its Partners as an individual, given the partnership as Landlord and the individual as Tenant, are deemed to be 2 distinct entities in Scots law[8].

(b) Premises

Any valid Lease must have a property that is the subject of use by the Tenant. It is strongly recommended that the full address and title number are narrated in the context of a title registered in the Land Register of Scotland. A plan is strongly recommended in circumstances where (a) the title is still recorded in the General Register of Sasines; or (b) the extent of the grant of the Lease involves only part and portion of the property owned by the Landlord. In the absence of specific and clear drafting, the question of the extent occupied by a Tenant can lead to disputes that will, ultimately, end up in litigation and shall depend on the facts and circumstances in each case. For example, in *United Kingdom Advertising Co V Glasgow Bag-Wash Laundry*[9] a right to use space for advertising in a post office, subject to the location being changed by the granter alone, was classed as a licence

---

7 Pages 60 and 61

8 See Mair V Wood 1948 SC 83

9 1926 SC 303

on the basis that there was no specific part of the heritable premises exclusively allocated to the grantee.

This can be compared and contrasted with *Brador Properties Limited V British Telecom Plc,*[10] where a reference to the use of part of an office, washroom and w.c. facilities, with access rights over common parts, all as may be designated by the granter of the Lease, was considered to be a sufficient description to create a Landlord and Tenant relationship in the circumstances. Furthermore, Lord Justice-Clerk Ross made it clear that "*I am not satisfied that, for there to be a lease, the subjects must remain the same throughout the duration of the agreement. Provided that parties are agreed as to a mechanism for determining what the subjects of the agreement is to be, there may still be a lease created*".[11] The fact that the tenant was given an entry card and key in the latter case was perhaps far more suggestive of exclusive possession being granted, tantamount to a Lease, which was arguably missing in the earlier case, where no such exclusive possession existed. This may or may not be definitive on its own but, in my view, it may have played an important factor in distinguishing both cases.

(c) Rent

The third constituent element is the payment of rent by the Tenant to the Landlord. If there is a grant of an agreement with no rent then the contract in question will not constitute a Lease. In *Mann V Houston*[12] a lease of 10 years, with no rent payable during the entire term, but which had a lump sum paid by the Tenant to the Landlord on the date of entry, was deemed not to be a Lease. As Lord President Clyde opined "*there is no provision of payment of a rent of any kind, however nominal, nor any acknowledgement that any rent has ever been paid, nor*

[10] 1992 SLT 490

[11] Page 496

[12] 1957 SLT 89

even an effectual discharge of the rent...... One or other of such provisions might have made the contract a lease binding on the granter and his heirs.... But none of them is present here........ and it becomes impossible to describe this contract as a lease as that word is understood in the law of Scotland........ In reality, in my opinion, the missives do nothing more than confer on the defender a personal right of occupancy of the garage for a certain period and subject to certain conditions........."[13]. There is no minimum figure of rent required by Scots Law, so a reference to the rent being expressed as "*£1 per annum, if demanded*" would be sufficient to constitute a rent obligation in a Lease. In *Shetland Islands Council V BP Petroleum Development Limited*[14] the council gave BP possession of the premises on the understanding that a lease would subsequently be put in place. Several licences were put in place during the period of occupation whilst the draft Lease was still to be adjusted and agreed. The Council asked the Court to determine the existence of a Lease between the parties and to fix a fair rent for the period of occupation by BP. In short, the Court refused to do so on the basis that the absence of a rent being paid was fatal to the constitution of a Lease between the parties. Furthermore, and on a separate note, Lord Cullen commented that "*I would have concluded that..... the licence was destructive of the pursuer's case as to the existence of a long lease between them and the defenders*"[15]. The refusal of a court to fix the rent was also demonstrated in the earlier case of *Gray V The University of Edinburgh*[16], where the parties were argued to have agreed to a payment of a reasonable and fair market rent. As Lord Justice-Clerk Thomson made clear, "*It is clear from what is said that the reference to a reasonable or fair market rent was nothing more than a convenient formula to be used as a guide to the negotiations. The parties went on to attempt to negotiate such a rent, but the negotiations broke down........*

[13] Pages 92 and 93

[14] 1990 SLT 82

[15] Page 91

[16] 1962 SC 157

I find it impossible on these averments to hold that there was consensus [in idem] as to rent......... Accordingly, there being no consensus as to rent, there was no contract of lease, and the pursuers case on this aspect is irrelevant."[17] The position in both the *Shetland Islands Council* case and the *Gray* case may have been decided differently if there was a specific mechanism, agreed by both parties, to determine how a dispute about rent would be determined. In the absence of such provisions, it is clear the Court will not step in and read between the lines to create a Lease between both parties.

(d) **Duration / Termination Date**

The duration of a lease, by statute, cannot exceed a total of 175 years.[18] In the absence of a specified termination date there is case law to imply that the term of a Lease is one year from the date of entry.[19] However, this is only on the strict understanding that all three of the other essential elements of a Lease are clearly established / determined. In the *Gray* case it was made clear that the failure to have an agreed and specified rent would not enable the parties to imply that the agreement was for an implied term of one year. If the parties had an agreed rent then the implied one year term would almost certainly have assisted in the determination of a Lease being in existence between the parties.

[17] Page 163

[18] s67 of the Abolition of Feudal Tenure etc (Scotland) Act 2000

[19] Gray V The University of Edinburgh 1962 SC 157

CHAPTER TWO

BREAK OPTIONS

Step 1 – Determine if a Break Option Exists or not

I'm sure none of you reading this chapter will be surprised to hear that the first place to look when you're instructed to serve a break option notice is the contract that sets out the rights and entitlement of each party – the Lease! Firstly, you should check that the break option actually exists and that the deadline for service has not, in fact, already passed.

A typical clause that I draft in my leases would say "***the Tenant [assuming this is a defined term] shall be entitled, but not bound, to terminate the lease on the 5th anniversary of the Date of Entry [assuming this is a defined term] upon providing written notice to the Landlord [assuming this is a defined term] of at least 6 months, time being of the essence.***" So, in terms of this clause, the break option, upon being exercised correctly, would terminate the Lease at the 5th anniversary of the Date of Entry. The definitions of the Date of Entry and the notice period should be carefully considered to ensure that there is still sufficient time to serve a break notice on the Landlord.

Step 2 – Requirements in the Method of Service of a Break Notice

The next step for any practitioner should be to work out how to notify the Landlord that the Tenant is exercising its break option. This is where the "Notice" provisions, typically found towards the end of the Lease, should be carefully checked in each instance. In general, I would distinguish between 2 forms of requirements in a clause of this nature.

As we will see, if the clause says that a certain manner of service has to be followed then it is called a prescriptive provision and, ultimately, this means that a failure to follow it is a breach of its requirements, prejudicing the early termination itself. For example, if a clause requires service by 1st Class Recorded Delivery only then it can be classed as prescriptive as there is only one means of service. Alternatively, if a clause sets out that there is more than one method of serving a Notice then it can be classed as a permissive (or non-prescriptive) provision. Such a clause then usually sets out how the service will be deemed to be successful – in other words even if the other party did not actually receive the break notice upon the permitted methods of service being followed. So, for example, if a Recorded Delivery notice is sent out and then returned by the Post Office because the addressee was not available and did not thereafter collect it then most modern clauses deem receipt by the recipient 48 hours from the date that it was posted. The deeming provision is, however, of great importance in the context of both timing and receipt. In *Gateway Assets Ltd v C.V. Panels Ltd*[20] there was a dispute between the parties about whether a break notice had been received by the Landlord. The case held, on the facts and evidence presented by the parties, that the break notice had not been sent. However, Lord Clark commented that such a deeming provision in the Notices section of the Lease is effectively treated as parties contracting out of the common law obligation on the Tenant to prove that the break notice letter was sent and received by the Landlord. If proof of sending could be demonstrated then the Landlord's failure to receive same would not prejudice the successful exercise of the break option. The Tenant in this case did not utilise Recorded Delivery and, as such, was left trying to prove a letter was sent by ordinary post in the context of quite strong evidence to the contrary from the Landlord showing its mail opening procedures. There was also evidence showing internal email exchanges on or around the last deadline for service advising that no break notice had been served by its Tenants. As Lord

20 2018 CSOH 48

Clark summarised "*deemed service could be achieved by complying with the provision. Otherwise, proof of receipt was required, but the evidential presumption....... can still be utilised for that purpose....... as the parties accepted, if deemed receipt under the lease provision cannot be relied upon, and if the presumption of receipt because of proof of sending is rebutted, there is a need to prove by other means that the notice was actually received, which of course was not done or attempted here.*"[21]

Step 3 – Sufficient Notice Must be Given where Time is of the Essence

It is not always possible, especially when dealing with clients, but it is best practice to ensure you are serving a break notice well in advance of the deadline.

In *Esson Properties Limited V Dresser UK Limited*[22] a break clause in a Lease of industrial premises in Aberdeen required the Tenant to provide the Landlord with not less than 9 months of notice prior to the specified break date. On 31st October 1995 the Tenant served a break notice to the Landlord, purporting to terminate the Lease at 31st July 1996, and the dispute between the parties was whether sufficient notice had been provided in terms of the Lease. Lord Penrose held that a reference to not less than 9 months of notice prior to a specified date "*has a well-defined meaning in law.... that on such an approach both the first day and the last day fall to be excluded in computing the period of uninterrupted time that must elapse between the giving of the notice and the expiry of the period for notice stipulated*". In other words, it is settled law to ignore the date of service and the final date of the period in calculating the period of notice that has actually been given. The Lease was, therefore, held to have continued beyond the early termination

[21] Paragraphs 67 and 68

[22] 1997 SC 304

date as insufficient notice had been given by the Tenant to the Landlord.

Step 4 – Determine who is the Landlord to serve the Notice on the Correct Party

I cannot emphasise enough that any practitioner should carry out a search to determine ownership of the leased premises immediately prior to the service of the notice. It is all fine and well to ask the client who the Landlord is, and to ask for a rent invoice, but it is dangerous to rely on clients to tell us every development that happens prior to the break notice leaving your office. In the context of a title in the Land Register, we should not stop at simply looking at the registered proprietor – we need to specifically check for any applications undergoing registration in case a transfer of title or sale has taken place in the run-up to the break date and has not emerged from the woods yet with its new title sheet. Once you have the title sheet and, having checked the applications undergoing registration, you need to also get into the habit of checking Companies House, where the Landlord is a Limited Company, to determine if there has been a change of name or, more importantly, a change of Registered Office. The Notices section of the Lease usually always requires that a notice is served on a Company at the Registered Office and, if it is determined that, at the point of service, the Notice has gone to a different address, then you will almost certainly find yourself in hot water in trying to prove successful service.

A case on point, demonstrating the importance of who the notice is served upon, is *Ben Cleuch Estates Limited V Scottish Enterprise*[23]. This case involved a Lease of Enterprise House in Dundee, where there was a break option in favour of the Tenant to terminate the Lease at any time before 2nd February 2005 upon written notice of at least one year.

[23] 2008 SC 252

The original company that owned the property was ultimately known as Bonnytoun Estates Limited. Bonnytoun then acquired a subsidiary company and decided to transfer the title to its subsidiary, originally known as Pacific Shelf 1145 Limited, and then the said subsidiary changed its name to Ben Cleuch Estates Limited. Whilst the transfer of ownership was intimated to the Tenant it was clear that the change of name had not been disclosed formally. It was clear from the evidence led that both the Parent Company and the Subsidiary both had the same Registered Office. The only share issued by the Subsidiary was owned by the Parent Company. Invoices for rent continued to be issued to the Tenant by Managing Agents that were, as specified on the invoices "*acting as agents of Bonnytoun Estates Limited*". Ben Cleuch were never specified as the principal in these invoices, although strangely they were mentioned in the property address section of the invoice. There was also evidence to suggest that a consent that was appropriate from Ben Cleuch had been issued by the Managing Agents on behalf of the said Bonnytoun Estates Limited. Anyway, I think you all know where this summary is going! The solicitors for the Tenants issued a break notice – the first one went to Bonnytoun Estates Limited at its Registered Office, and a further break notice went to an address that had been supplied by the agents as a point of contact for a Mr Scott Cairns, a Director of Bonnytoun, but which was a separate address in Linlithgow. Upon expiry of the break date the solicitors for Ben Cleuch advised their Tenant that they were of the view that the Notices were invalid because they had been addressed to a party that was not the Landlord and wanted to hold the Tenant to adhere to the Lease to its natural expiry date. The issues before the Court were therefore whether the Notices were valid to exercise the break option and, if not, whether there was sufficient scope to argue that the operation of personal bar, due to the conduct of the agents, was sufficient to prohibit Bonnytoun from arguing that the break notice was defective. Lord Macfadyen held that "*a notice addressed to a party other than the landlord and sent to the registered office of that other party cannot be regarded as a notice given to the landlords.......that the break notice sent to [the Registered Office] ultimately found its way into the hands of Mr Cairns is in our view of no assistance to the defenders. Clause FOURTH concentrates on the party to whom the notice is given, not the party who may ultimately receive it...... That he [Mr Cairns] happened also to be a director of Ben Cleuch and thus acquired knowledge of the notice and was able to react to it in that capacity does not, in our opinion, convert a notice given to Bonnytoun into a notice given to Ben Cleuch."*[24]

So, with the first part of the argument thrown out, was there merit in suggesting that Scottish Enterprise were justified in their belief that Bonnytoun were the landlords and that they had acted in reliance on that belief to their prejudice, namely by giving the break notice to Bonnytoun, leaving Ben Cleuch personally barred from objecting to the defective notice? The requirements of a successful personal bar argument were quoted from the judgement of Lord Birkenhead in *Gatty V Maclaine*[25], known as estoppel in England. Lord Birkenhead summarised "*where A has by his words or conduct justified B in believing that a certain state of facts exists, and B has acted upon such belief to his prejudice, A is not permitted to affirm against B that a different state of facts existed at the same time*[26]". A second quote from Lord Denning was used to affirm this from the case of *Sidney Bolsom Investment Trust Limited V E Karmios & Co (London) Limited*[27] summarising that "*in order to work as an estoppel, the representation must be clear and unequivocal, it must be intended to be acted on, and in fact acted on. And when I say it must be intended to be acted upon I would add that a man must be taken to intend what a reasonable person would understand him to intend. In short the representation must be made in such circumstances*

[24] Paragraphs 60 and 63

[25] 1921 SC (HL) 1

[26] Page 7

[27] 1956 1 QB 529

as to convey an invitation to act on it"[28]. Lord Macfadyen then took these comments a step further and summarised that, to be successful with an argument of personal bar, the representation must be such that "*a reasonable man would regard it as intended to be believed and relied upon*[29]". Lord Macfadyen held that it was a reasonable inference from the invoices in all the circumstances to assume that Bonnytoun was the Landlord and the argument of personal bar was, in this case, successful.

In another similar situation, *Batt Cables Plc V Spencer Business Parks Limited,*[30] Lord Hodge was asked to determine a dispute between a Landlord and Tenant over the operation of a break notice served by the Tenant. The property was an industrial premises at Lochend Industrial Estate in Newbridge. The difference here was that the parent Company of the Landlord owner, Spencer Holdings Plc, had written to Batt Cables Plc upon the acquisition of the Estate by its subsidiary to say that it had in excess of 500 tenants and specifically told the Tenant to contact Joe Dempsey for "*Tenancy Issues – rent reviews, lease renewals, applications for landlord's consent, occupation enquiries*". The question was whether such correspondence could be treated as authority to entitle the Tenant to send the break notice to Mr Dempsey as an authorised agent for the Landlord. On the basis of the proof lead by the Tenants, Lord Hodge found in favour of the Tenant. In his judgement he comments that "*for a notice given to an agent to be valid, it had to be established that the agent had authority to receive it. To demonstrate that the agent was so authorised often means that the person seeking to uphold the notice has to show that the agent was a general agent in the sense that the agent has authority to do anything in relation to the subject matter of the agency….. I accept that in the absence of express authority creating a general agency, there must be clear evidence to support*

[28] Pages 540 and 541

[29] Paragraph 87

[30] 2010 SLT 860

the inference of such agency....... there is nothing in the case law to which I was referred which supports the view that an agent who is charged by his principal to receive and process all correspondence relating to the principal does not have power to receive a break notice from a tenant of the principal."[31] In trying to compare this to Ben Cleuch and summarising the position overall, it would be my opinion that a notice addressed to anyone other than the actual Landlord will be defective – and cannot be valid – unless it can be proven that the person or organisation who the notice has been sent to is an agent for the actual Landlord. It is relatively clear that it has to be an agent that is empowered to process all correspondence on behalf of the principal – and not simply a solicitor or surveyor that is instructed in respect of certain stand-alone professional matters.

You may be surprised to learn that the question of authorised agency is not only relevant for the recipient of the notice but also the party that is serving the notice if it is anyone other than the Tenant. In *Hexstone Holdings Limited V AHC Westlink Limited*[32], which affirmed the earlier decision in *Lemmerbell Limited and Matthew Fraser Limited V Brittania LAS Direct Limited*[33], a Notice was held to be invalid because it had been served by the parent company of the actual Tenant. Critically, there was no evidence that the parent company was authorised to act as agent on behalf of the subsidiary. The explanation for this stance is that a Landlord needs to have certainty in knowing whether a break is being triggered or not, and it is not the role of the Landlord to go and make enquiries on whether a 3rd party serving a notice is actually authorised by the principal to do so. Indeed the judgement comments that "*the notepaper on which the notice was written..... was not [that] of the original tenant...... once that point is appreciated I find it impossible to see how Hexstone could safely have relied on the Notice in*

[31] Paragraphs 36 and 37

[32] 2010 EWHC 1280

[33] 1999 L&TR 102

the knowledge that it would be binding on the true principal. For all Hexstone knew.... the lease could perhaps have been assigned....... the problem for AHC of course is that [an argument of general agency] is not established and that is why the Notice becomes confusing to the reasonable recipient....."[34] The outcome of this is a timely reminder, to all practitioners as well as any other agent sending such a notice, that they need to expressly say in the break option that the sender is instructed to act on behalf of the Tenant, as agent, and a failure to do so could lead to someone arguing that there is nothing on the face of the break notice confirming that it is served by an authorised agent of the Tenant.

Step 5 – Carefully consider any Conditions attached to the Exercise of the Break Option

What about extra requirements that are introduced by the Landlord and/or the drafter? For example, and more prominently since the recession around 2007/2008, it is fairly normal for Landlords' to introduce conditions attaching to the break option granted to the Tenant in order to make early termination as difficult as possible. We are going to review a number of the cases associated with conditions attaching to break options. It is important that such conditions are carefully reviewed and complied with as, if the break is entirely dependent on compliance with said conditions, then a failure to do so could completely prejudice the exercise of the break.

In *The Hotgroup Plc V The Royal Bank of Scotland Plc as Trustee of Schroder Exempt Property Unit Trust*[35] the Lease entitled the Tenant to terminate early, at 3rd July 2010, upon 9 months of written notice. One of the clauses in the Lease specifically provided that "*during such period as the reversion to this Lease is vested in the trustee [Schroder] no*

[34] Paragraph 44

[35] 2010 EWHC 1241

notice will be deemed to be validly served on the Landlord unless a copy of the Notice is also served on Schroder Property Investment Management Limited......"[36]. Unfortunately for the Tenant, the duplicate notice to the trustee was not served until 19th November 2009, clearly in breach of the prior requirement of 9 months' of written notice. During the case, it was clear that the Tenant's agents were vigorously cross-examining the recipient of the Landlord's notice in the hope of gaining something to discredit his overall evidence. The deputy judge commented that "*it became apparent that the purpose of subjecting Mr Meredith to cross-examination was to elicit answers from him which would enable THL to seek leave to amend their pleaded case.... that there had, after all, been proper service..... because RBS had in fact passed on a copy of the notice served on them [to the Trustee]...... I refused leave to amend.... and indicated I would give my reasons in this judgement.... the application was hopeless.........THL have failed to comply with the terms of the break clause and it has not validly been exercised. The claim must therefore be dismissed and RBS entitled to a declaration that the break clause option has not been complied with*"[37].

In a similar vein, a break option is for the benefit of "the Tenant" and the definition of the Tenant in the Lease will usually always include any successors and assignees. If something is personal to a Tenant, however, then the Landlord's solicitor would usually try and keep it out of the Lease. Tenants, traditionally, don't like that suggestion because the concession or right will be lost if the Landlord is sequestrated or if a company goes into receivership, administration or liquidation. I can recall in many transactions the compromise was to put wording in the Lease that made it quite clear that such a right was personal to a particular individual or entity. It would be along the lines of "*declaring always that in so far as the Tenant remains the said Amir M Ismail he shall be entitled but not bound to terminate the Lease on the 5th*

[36] Paragraph 4

[37] Paragraph 11

anniversary of the Date of Entry upon written notice of at least 6 months". In *Aviva Life and Pensions UK Limited V Linpac Mouldings Limited*[38] a subsequent assignee of the personal break option sought to get declarator that it was entitled to the exercise of the break option, even though it was clear from the wording that it was a personal right of the original Tenant. No surprises here – it was held that the right was personal and was incapable of being utilised by any other party. It follows that, if you are acting for a client in the assignation of a Lease that has a personal break option in favour of the assignor or original tenant, you need to specifically add wording in your assignation and variation to say the break option can be utilised by your client – or even easier – create a completely new break option. If it says the right is not binding on successor tenants then I cannot see any scope to suggest it will survive a subsequent assignation.

When drafting break options with conditions you need to be clear in determining what they are conditional upon and, if it is compliance with the rest of the obligations of the Lease (monetary and/or non-monetary), whether it is at the point of service of the notice or the break date (or both). In *Trygort (No 2) Limited V UK Home Finance Limited*[39] the drafting was even more questionable because the lease specified that a break notice could not be served by the Tenant if it had been in breach of its obligations to the Landlord. Did this mean that if there had been any breach during the term the break option was effectively and permanently forfeited or, alternatively, did it mean that there must be no breaches at the date of the break? The court heard that the earlier English case of *Bass Holdings Limited V Morton Music Limited*[40] established that spent breaches did not destroy the tenant's break option in these circumstances but subsisting breaches did. It was also held that there were no outstanding breaches at the

38 2010 EWCA CIV 395

39 2008 CSIH 56

40 1988 1 CH 493

point of operation of the break. The Court held in favour of the Tenant and, in using *Bass Holdings* as a relevant and persuasive case, determined that the commercially sensible construction of the provision was to consider breaches at the point of the termination of the Lease by virtue of the break option. Indeed, the judgement in *Bass Holdings* was very compelling, especially the comment from Lord Justice Kerr that "*absolute and precise compliance by the tenant with every single covenant throughout the period of the lease prior to the operative date is virtually impossible of attainment. If this were required as a condition precedent then the option would in practice be worthless or merely at the option of the Landlord.*"[41] It follows that if you are instructed to draft something along these lines then it needs to be crystal clear and unambiguous – and from the Tenant's perspective it should be resisted resolutely.

Another element of conditionality to a break option was found in *Arlington Business Parks GP Limited V Scottish & Newcastle Limited.*[42] Here, a Lease of 1 and 2 Broadway Park in Edinburgh contained a break option. The Tenant was entitled to terminate upon written notice of at least 12 months as long as it was not in breach of any of its obligations under the Lease at the date of service and/or the termination date. So quite a high benchmark – its compliance at both service of the notice and the subsequent break date itself. The Tenants accepted that they had not complied with their repairing obligation at the point of service of the notice. They argued that such breaches were capable of being addressed in the supervening period – which physically is true if not legally – and they then set about spending the best part of £1.3m on putting the property into a spic and span condition at the break date. The Landlord naturally said thank you very much – but then proceeded to say you're staying for the remainder of the term because the break notice was ineffective as a result of your breach of

[41] Page 518

[42] 2014 CSOH 77

the repairing obligation! The Landlord was successful in determining that the Tenant had to be in compliance with all of its obligations at both dates, and an attempt by the Tenant to suggest that it was only in respect of material obligations was unsuccessful because the wording did not support that. If you think this through carefully then the opposite would also lead to the same outcome – if all repairs and payments are implemented at the point of service but rent is outstanding at the break date then the case is authority for cancelling the removal men.

Could we do anything to avoid a situation where the Landlord serves a Schedule of Dilapidations the week before the last service date of a break notice? Or sends out a common charges invoice requiring payment within 14 days on the 16th day before the last service date of a break notice? The answer is yes – you can either:

1. Play it safe and try to delete the conditionality part of the clause completely;

2. Restrict the conditionality to be in respect of rent only; or

3. Revise the wording to specify that the Landlord shall not be entitled to demand payment of any sums outwith rent or serve a schedule of dilapidations in the period immediately 14 days and 2 months in each instance, respectively, prior to the said break date, and which shall not prejudice the Tenant's break. This should give the Tenant a fighting chance of adhering to the terms of the Lease without the Landlord being tactical and throwing banana skins around the service and break dates.

Another really interesting conditional break option case is *Riverside Park Limited V NHS Property Services Limited.*[43] In this case, the NHS were tenants in a 10-year FRI Lease and had a break option at year 5,

---

[43] 2016 EWHC 1313

which was conditional upon vacant possession being given to the Landlord at the break date. The Tenant had obtained Landlord's consent to carry out a fit-out at the premises and this was documented within a typical Licence for Works (aka a Licence to Alter in England). The Tenant's fit-out generally consisted of a kitchen and a series of non-structural partitions to arrange a number of small rooms. The Tenant served a notice to break the Lease timeously but left the property without reinstating the premises to its condition before the works were carried out (a typical obligation within any Licence for Works / Licence to Alter). The Landlord argued that this failure amounted to a failure to return vacant possession and the break should be ineffective. In England, the question turned on whether the alterations were classed as moveable items (Tenant possessions) or were now forming part of the Premises (thus acceded to the premises). The nature of the works were not classed as being of a particularly permanent nature and, as such, the Court held that vacant possession being returned to the Landlord was intended to be a reference to vacant possession once all works it had carried out had been reinstated, as required by the Licence for Works / Licence to Alter. This meant that the break notice was ineffective and the Tenant was stuck for another 5 years. Quite a costly decision for the Tenant and, whilst it is persuasive in Scotland, you would not need to look far to find a number of instances where Scottish courts have followed English precedent in upholding an argument. In modern practice, we have to ensure that we emphasise to clients that they either do all reinstatement works prior to a break option being exercised or we add in wording in the Lease at the outset to say that a failure to remove the Tenant's fit-out will not be deemed as fatal to the operation of the break option itself. There were similar issues in the case of *NYK Logistics (UK) Limited V Ibrend Estates BV*[44] and it was held that, if a break clause requires vacant possession at the break date, then a failure to do so will completely invalidate the early termination of the Lease. The Lease in question was a 2 year term at

[44] 2011 EWCA CIV 683

£278k and, having served a break notice in September 2008 to terminate the Lease on 3rd April 2009, the Tenant found itself with a Schedule of Dilapidations served by the Landlord at 11th March 2009. The parties subsequently entered into a dialogue, where it was suggested, but clearly not agreed, that the Tenant would need more time beyond the break date to complete all wants of repair. As it happens, all but two items were done by 3rd April 2009, and the final two were completed on 9th April 2009. To be absolutely clear – the break was conditional upon vacant possession being given back to the Landlord but did **not** require all monetary or non-monetary obligations under the Lease to be implemented by that date (meaning the Landlord would have a traditional claim for dilapidations after the break date termination if all works were not completed by 3rd April 2009). In what was a very clear and critical passage, not only setting out the logic but also how this very situation could have been avoided, Lord Justice Rimer commented that "*the concept of vacant possession in the present context is not, I consider, complicated. It means what it does in every domestic and commercial sale in which there is an obligation to give vacant possession on completion. It means that at the moment that vacant possession is required to be given, the property is empty of people and that the purchaser is able to assume and enjoy immediate and exclusive possession, occupation and control of it. It must also be empty of chattels, although the obligation in respect is likely only to be breached if any chattels left in the property substantially prevent or interfere with the enjoyment of the right of possession of a substantial part of the property...... [The Tenant] ought to have known that...... its only safe course was to move everyone out of the warehouse on Friday, including its security guard....... It could then have contacted Ibrend on Monday April 6th and asked it whether it would permit it to return to the warehouse as its licensee in order to complete the outstanding works...... It did not <u>have</u> to carry out [the works] as a condition of the exercise of the break option. It <u>wanted</u> to do them in order to avoid the prospect of a subsequent claim for damages in excess of its own cost of doing them. Its wish in that respect was also no justification for giving* *itself an extension of time for the giving of possession."*[45] The case is clear authority for prioritising vacant possession where it is a specific condition of the break option. If there is a mutual desire to extend the deadline then it should be formally documented to avoid the break option being invalidated as a result of a failure to deliver vacant possession.

Step 6 – Is there an automatic right to apportionment of rent at the break date?

So, we get to the stage where a notice is drafted, successfully served and any conditions attached to same are addressed timeously. Lets say the break date sits in the middle of 2 rent payment dates in terms of the Lease. If the Tenant doesn't pay the rent on the rent payment date before the break date then we already know it is in breach and if this is a condition of the early break then the attempt to exercise the break is ineffective. Is the Tenant entitled to a refund of the pre-paid rent attributable from the date of the break date to the day before the next quarter date?

This was the question that arose in the case of *Marks and Spencer Plc v BNP Paribas Securities Services Trust Company (Jersey) Limited.*[46] M & S were tenants in a building known as the Point in Paddington Basin, London. They sought to exercise their right to terminate the Lease at 24th January 2012, having paid the full quarter of rent on the English payment day (Christmas Day in 2011). You may wonder why they raised an action to seek to recover the balance of rent for just over 2 months? The rent in this Lease was in excess of £1.2m per annum, exclusive of VAT and service charges. They had to make the payment because the break option was conditional upon all payments and non-monetary obligations being implemented at the break date. There was

45 Paragraphs 44 to 47

46 2015 UKSC 72

no specific clause requiring the Landlord to reimburse the sums attributable beyond the break date, but M & S were purporting to argue that there was an implied term in the Lease enabling them to recover the sums in question. The judgement set out that terms would only be implied in leases if, as set out in *Arnold V Britton*[47], they were "*necessary to give business efficacy*" to the contract. Lord Neuberger acknowledged that, if the Landlord was able to retain the sum, then it would be a 100% windfall for the Landlord and unfairly prejudicial to the Tenant. There was no common law entitlement to an apportionment of rent in general terms, and Lord Neuberger also commented that, if the rent was payable in arrears, then the Landlord would have suffered the loss. In the circumstances, Lord Neuberger found in favour of the Landlord, commenting that "*it would be wrong to attribute to a Landlord and a tenant, particularly when they have entered into a full and professionally drafted lease, an intention that the Tenant should receive an apportioned part of the rent payable and paid in advance, when the non-apportionability of such rent has been so long and clearly established. Given that it is so clear that the effect of the case law is that rent payable and paid in advance can be retained by the Landlord, save in very exceptional circumstances (eg where the contract could not work or would lead to an absurdity) express words would be needed before it would be right to imply a term to the contrary...... indeed the result cannot be said to be commercially or otherwise absurd....*"[48] The important thing to note here is that where a break date lies outwith the payment dates in question then you should necessarily add express wording to enable the Tenant to recover any payments attributable to the period beyond the break date within a specified timescale after lease termination. A failure to do so would result in no grounds to insist upon repayment, because the legal position would deem the Tenant to have carefully weighed up the early termination of the Lease

[47] See the 7 steps of interpretation set out therein – Arnold V Britton 2015 2 WLR 1593

[48] Paragraphs 50 and 51

against its loss of advance payments in determining its decision to serve the notice.

Step 7 – Protection against Errors of Content rather than Service

We have looked at the cases determining that a notice served on the wrong party is invalid unless it can be shown to be served on an authorised agent of the actual Landlord. There is nothing that can remedy this – even if the wrong recipient shares the same Registered Office or officers of the Company – or even if it can be shown that the notice ended up with the true Landlord. So, in the last part of this chapter, I would like to wrap matters up by looking at the position where the Notice has been served on the correct Landlord but contains errors of content.

The leading case here is *Mannai Investment Co Limited V Eagle Star Assurance.*[49] This was a case where the lease permitted the Tenant to terminate the Lease at the 3rd anniversary of the Date of Entry. Whilst the notice was served timeously, and to the correct party, the notice itself had the wrong date – namely it said 12th January 1995 instead of 13th January 1995. Not exactly error of the century you might think, but it could either be considered as close enough to let both parties know what they meant or, in adopting a strict approach, it was purporting to exercise a break option on a date that the Lease did not permit.

Lord Steyn summarised the position quite succinctly when he said "*the question is not how the Landlord understood the notices. The construction of the notices must be approached objectively. The issue is how a reasonable recipient would have understood the notices. And in considering this question the notices must be construed taking into account the relevant objective contextual scene. First, in respect of contracts and contractual notices*

[49] 1997 AC 749

the contextual scene is always relevant. Secondly, what is admissible as a matter of the rules of evidence under this heading is what is arguably relevant. The real question is what evidence of surrounding circumstances may ultimately be allowed to influence the question of interpretation. Thirdly, the enquiry is objective, the question is what reasonable person, circumstanced as the actual parties were, would have had in mind. It follows that one cannot ignore that a reasonable recipient of the notices would have had in the forefront of his mind the terms of the leases.... It is important not to lose sight of the purpose of a notice under a break clause. It serves one purpose only – to inform the Landlord that the Tenant has decided to determine the lease in accordance with the right reserved......I venture to suggest that that it is obvious that a reasonable recipient would have appreciated that the tenant wishes to determine the lease on the 3rd anniversary date of the leases but wrongly described it as the 12th instead of the 13th"[50]. It would appear that the test boils down to what the reasonable recipient with background knowledge would have interpreted the notice to say. As Lord Clyde summarises in the same case – "*where a notice of termination complies precisely and unambiguously with the provision which empowers the sending of the notice then its validity should not be questioned. Where the terms of the notice do not altogether accord with the provisions of the contract that may or may not render the notice unenforceable. The problem then may come to be one of finding a fair and reasonable construction of the notice. But there can be cases where the validity of the notice cannot be saved by any construction and will have to be regarded as valid.*[51]"

The invalidation of a break notice due to content errors appears to be a question of degree and circumstances, depending on the wording of the notice and the terms of the Lease itself. The application of the reasonable recipient test was demonstrated well in the case of *Tyco Fire & Integrated Solutions (UK) Limited V Regent Quay Development*

[50] Pages 767, 768 and 769

[51] Page 781

Company Limited.[52] In this case a break notice was served by the Tenant's agents but the premises were referred to as "Units 3 and 4" instead of "Units 1, 3 and 4". In effect, the Lease was varied during the term to extend the definition of "Premises" to bring in Unit 1 but neither the variation or the new unit featured in the break notice. Lord Tyre commented, in finding in favour of the Tenant, that "*I am satisfied that the reasonable recipient would not have been perplexed in any way by the error in the letter heading. The operative element of the notice is sufficiently clear and unambiguous to avoid any such perplexity and the fact that the ingenuity of lawyers can suggest theoretical ambiguities is not to the point*[53]". And, in *AWD Chase De Vere Wealth Management Limited V Melville Street Properties Limited*[54] a break notice served narrating the wrong name of the Tenant, which had subsequently changed twice since the original Lease was put in place, was found not to invalidate the exercise of the break option. As Lord Glennie explained, "*it is important to emphasise that the notice is not to be interpreted as though received by a stranger to the contract, however reasonable that stranger may be. It is treated as received by a reasonable Landlord in the position of the landlord under this lease. Lord Steyn makes this clear in Mannai. In a case such as the present, the Landlord will know of the terms of the Lease. He will know – and it is in fact clear from the terms of the letter of 4th February 2009 from his own solicitors that he did know – that the tenants named in the Lease have changed their name... He will also know that he has not consented to any assignation of the Lease...... I do not consider that the terms of the letter, unfortunate though the description......... was, would have caused a reasonable Landlord in the position of the defenders to doubt that notice was being served on behalf of the actual tenants.*[55]"

---

52 2016 CSOH 97

53 Paragraph 16

54 2010 SCLR 521

55 Paragraphs 8 and 10

It is clear that break options have given litigators a lot of work over the years, and whilst litigators will always find loopholes and angles to develop the law, I hope that the foregoing will assist you in minimising the opportunity for errors and invalidation of a break notice.

CHAPTER THREE

IRRITANCY – MONETARY BREACHESS

In its simplest form, irritancy is a legal right entitling a Landlord to terminate a Lease as a result of breach(es) by its Tenant during the term. The law of irritancy for commercial leases presently consists of a blend of statute (setting a minimum framework of protection for Tenants no matter what the Lease says) and, subsequently, a significant number of cases, which have interpreted, and then determined how the legislation will be applied in specific circumstances. The breaches leading to irritancy can be categorised as either monetary or non-monetary in their nature and, as such, it seems this distinction would be a logical split in this book in order to look at the necessary requirements.

If a Lease does not have an irritancy clause then, at common law, the Landlord can only irritate for monetary breaches that are tantamount to 2 years of unpaid rent[56]. No modern Landlord, even those with a great degree of patience, will wait 2 years for an income to appear. As such, and in most instances, a Lease will have express wording setting out the right of irritancy ("conventional irritancy"), as well as appropriate timescales, and the circumstances enabling the option at the instance of the Landlord.

Clauses will quite frequently require a notice of irritancy to be served on a heritable creditor of the Tenant's long leasehold interest and/or any floating charge holder to enable the creditor in question to step in and address the breach to preserve the value of the Lease. Irrespective

[56] This can be traced back to the Act of Sederunt of December 14 1756 (C.A.S.L xv 5)

of the specific wording, the Law Reform (Miscellaneous Provisions) (Scotland) Act 1985 applies a benchmark protection for Tenants in commercial leases, which cannot be contracted out of. Section 4 of the said Act deals with monetary breaches and provides, under subsection (1), that a clause enabling a Landlord to irritate a Lease for a monetary breach cannot be exercised until the statutory requirements have been met. Subsection (2) provides that the Landlord must serve a Notice on the Tenant requiring the Tenant to make payment of the outstanding sum and setting out that a failure to do so within the specified time frame may lead to the Lease being terminated at the expiry of the timeframe in question. The timeframe in question is narrated in Subsection (3) as being the greater of (a) 14 days from service of the Notice on the Tenant (NB not the date of the Notice itself); and (b) such other period specified in the Lease commencing, again, on the date of service of the Notice (but which cannot be less than 14 days)[57]. Subsection (4) sets out that the Notice, which, in practice, is commonly referred to as the "*Notice of Threatened Irritancy*", must be served on the Tenant by Recorded Delivery.

A number of cases have arisen following challenges of various Notices of Threatened Irritancy. In *Scott V Muir*[58] Sheriff Principal Stephen found the Notice served by the Landlord to be defective because it did not specify a period for payment of the outstanding sums to be made, as set out in Subsection (2) of the 1985 Act. In delivering the judgement the Sheriff Principal comments "*paragraph (i) of the notice fails to require the tenant to make payment within any specified period. There is no mention of a deadline or time limit in that part of the notice which*

[57] The introduction of emergency legislation in April 2020, namely the Coronavirus (Scotland) Act 2020, following the outbreak of the global pandemic known as coronavirus, has extended the timeframe for irritancy of a commercial lease for monetary breaches from 14 days to 14 weeks – see paragraph 7 of Schedule 7 of the 2020 Act. This is likely to remain in force until such time as the pandemic subsides, in which instance it is likely the extended timeframe will cease to apply, and the original terms of the 1985 Act will apply once again.

[58] 2012 HOUS LR 20

is intended to set out the requirements on the tenant which he must comply with to avoid the lease coming to an end by way of irritancy. Section 4(3) of the Act is prescriptive about that."[59] A second defect in the Notice was also upheld, namely "*clearly the tenant cannot know what the landlord's understanding of the rent arrears is unless he stipulates the dates from which the rent is due and unpaid. That would hardly be an onerous obligation on the Landlord......... It would not appear to give sufficient time, however, for detailed discussion or discovery as to periods of default and it appears to me therefore that for the notice to be effective it should specify the periods from which the rent arrears arise.*"[60]

This case, however, conflicts with another decision in similar circumstances, namely on the necessity of the Landlord specifying the periods from which the arrears have arisen. In *Inverclyde Council V McCloskey t/a Prince of Wales Bar*[61] Sheriff Principal Murray commented that "*I do not share her [Sheriff Principal Stephen's] view that in order to address the mischief which s4 of the Act was introduced to remove, that specification of period for which the rent arrears are said to arise requires to be read in...... While I can see that there would be merit in providing more explanation in the notice as to the basis for the calculation of the sum due I do not consider that to be required by the statute........I read s4 (2) of the Act as laying down the minimum requirements of an adequate notice. It does not prescribe any form which the notice should take, or confine the notice to contain only the requirement to pay and the statement that if payment is not made within the time provided the lease may be terminated.*[62]"

In the absence of these conflicting decisions being distinguished, it would be safest for practitioners sending Notices of Threatened

---

[59] Paragraph 41

[60] Paragraph 43

[61] 2015 SLT (Sh Ct) 57

[62] Paragraphs 66, 74 and 75.

Irritancy to specify the outstanding sum in the body of the Notice and referring to a further Statement of Account. The Statement would show sums payable and dates in one column and payments, if any, received in the debit column, thus showing precisely how the arrears have accumulated at the date of the Notice itself (or such other specified date in advance). This will ensure that the sum and the periods of default are clearly part of the Notice and will avoid the purported irritancy being challenged at a later date by the Tenant's solicitors. Personally, I am inclined to agree with Sheriff Principal Murray, but I cannot say everyone else would not follow Sheriff Principal Stephen's view in subsequent cases.

In *Tawne Overseas Holdings Limited V the Firm of Newmiln Farm*[63] a notice was held to be defective due to the period for payment specifying that it was from the date of the actual Notice and not the date of service, being contrary to the prescriptive terms of s4 of the Act. In *Edinburgh Tours Limited V Diaman Singh*[64], it was held that the terms of the 1985 Act are a minimum threshold to be applied. If the parties have wording in the Notices section of the Lease providing service is sufficient in a certain manner unless shown to the contrary by the Tenant, (in other words permitting the Tenant to lead evidence that it did not receive the Notice) then, upon doing so, the Landlord's attempt at irritancy will not be successful. And in *Shetland Leasing & Property Developments Limited V Malcolm Alexander Younger*[65] it was held that a Notice that did not narrate the amount of interest payable on the rent was not invalid. Sheriff Mann commented that "*I have concluded that that the obligation as regards interest in this case is to pay it within a reasonable period after payment of the rent. It is an obligation in its own right. In this case...... the obligation was not exigible as at the date of service of the section 4 Notice. It follows that it was not necessary,*

63 2008 CSOH 12

64 2012 Hous LR 15

65 2014 Hous LR 9

or appropriate, that the notice demanded payment of the interest. The validity of the Notice cannot be attacked on the basis that it includes a matter, namely a reference to interest, which goes beyond what is required by section 4."[66] In many circles, including my own firm, it is our practice not to include interest on outstanding rent in order to limit the possibility of the Notice being challenged in the event of irritancy taking place after the specified period.

There is, of course, nothing to prohibit the Landlord sending out an invoice for the interest once payment is received from the Tenant for the original arrears. At this junction a far more accurate calculation can be carried out, namely interest on the number of days from the due date to the date of payment (depending on the terms of the Lease). It is, however, worthwhile mentioning, on the question of interest, that there is authority to suggest irritating a Lease for interest on arrears may not be permissible. In *Whitbread Group Plc V Goldapple Limited*[67] it was affirmed, in following the earlier case of *Aubrey Investments Limited V D S Crawford Limited (in receivership)*[68] that a Landlord pursuing irritancy for insignificant sums of money may amount to oppression. Lord Penrose was cited in *Aubrey Investments Limited* as commenting that "*Impropriety of conduct on the part of the Landlord is of the essence of oppression. A characteristic of improper conduct is invoking a contractual provision to procure an unfair consequence to the Tenant. The Landlord's motive will not of itself instruct a relevant case of oppression.*"[69] In using this quote as a framework for his comments, Lord Drummond Young goes on to say that where "*the amount of interest involved was trivial in the context of the rent due under the Lease........ [and] where...... there is a clear willingness to pay and also some doubt as to the precise amount due, I consider that the use of irritancy*

[66] Paragraphs 22 and 23

[67] 2005 SCLR 263

[68] 1998 SLT 628

[69] Page 634

for non-payment of a trivial amount would amount to oppressive conduct."[70]

The case of *CIN Properties Limited V Dollar Land (Cumbernauld) Limited*[71] also clarified, in taking the question of oppression in irritancy of a Lease a step further, through Lord Justice-Clerk Ross's passages, that "*I am not persuaded that a landlord who has been indulgent to a tenant in the past about late payment of rent can be said to be acting oppressively if he subsequently requires the tenant to comply with the provisions in the lease regarding payment of rent. Indeed when the whole history of past payment of rent is considered, the only reasonable inference is that the pursuers, far from acting oppressively, had behaved leniently towards the defenders so far as prompt payment of rent is concerned.*"[72] The case also re-affirmed that (a) oppression is the sole means of purging an irritancy for non-payment of rent[73]; and (b) a sublease will terminate upon the irritancy of the corresponding head lease, irrespective of whether a monetary or non-monetary breach, the wider background, and specific set of circumstances. In this instance, the subtenants were left attempting to enter into new agreements directly with the Landlord. The only comfort that a Subtenant can seek to protect its own interest, if the Head Lease is irritated, is to enter into an Irritancy Protection Agreement directly with the Landlord. This will require the Landlord to grant a new lease on terms *mutatis mutandis* for the remainder of the unexpired term of the original Sublease[74], albeit entirely at the Subtenant's expense. In a subsequent appeal the Court refused to provide the Tenant with a right to compensation under the laws of unjustified enrichment, on the basis that both parties to the

[70] Paragraph 56

[71] 1992 SC (HL) 104

[72] Page 110

[73] Lord Jauncey of Tullichettle at page 122

[74] See PSG Legal Website – www.psg-legal.co.uk – for an excellent style of Irritancy Protection Agreement

head lease clearly agreed to the inclusion of an irritancy clause, and it was not for the Courts to step in and over-rule the prior express commercial terms.[75]

In *Ashford and Thistle Securities LLP V Kerr*[76] it was determined that a purchaser of a property with a commercial Lease in place, where there are arrears of rent by the Tenant at the date of purchase, can only serve a Notice of Threatened Irritancy if it either (a) requires the outstanding sums to be paid to the original Landlord (the Seller); or (b) sets out the basis upon which the sums should be paid to the new Landlord as Purchaser. It is notable that the new Landlord in this case did neither, and no prior intimation of change of ownership was sent to the Tenant, meaning the Notice from a party the Tenant had never heard of fell below the s4 requirements of the 1985 Act (in that it was unclear how the tenant was to comply within the specified period).[77] And, in a similar case, *Life Association of Scotland Limited V Blacks Leisure Group Plc*[78] it was held that a Purchaser of a property, where a notice of irritancy was served by the Seller as former Landlord, would, in order to rely on the Notice to subsequently obtain a decree for possession, "*require to obtain an express assignation of it [the Notice]. Without an assignation, they cannot have the benefit of the Notice*"[79]. The suggestion in the case itself was that it would be safest to bring any action for the recovery of possession in joint names of the Seller and Purchaser.

Whilst we touch upon the actions of predecessor Landlords, in *What Every Woman Wants (1971) Limited V Wholesale Paint and Wallpaper Co Limited*[80] it was held that the failure of a former Landlord to

---

75 1998 SC (HL) 90

76 2007 SLT (Sh Ct) 60

77 See Paragraph 11

78 1989 SLT 674

79 Lord Justice-Clerk Ross at page 170

80 1984 SLT 133

exercise irritancy on a number of prior occasions where there were arrears did not taint the right of a subsequent purchaser, as new Landlord, to irritate the Lease, and that it was an essential requirement of personal bar that the conduct in question was not attributable to a 3rd party as it was in this instance.

A relatively recent case, *Kodak Processing Limited V Shoredale Limited*[81] clarified that the service of Notices were prescriptive under s4(4) of the 1985 Act. In other words, subsection 4 required service by Recorded Delivery post, and, in using Sheriff Officers, the requirements of the Act had not been followed and the attempt to irritate a Lease using Sheriff Officers was invalid. This decision has attracted criticism in many quarters given it was common knowledge the Royal Mail were on strike at the time of the service of the Notice by Sheriff Officers.

It is possible for conduct of parties, subsequent to irritancy being effected, to cancel the irritancy. The case of *HMV Fields Properties Limited V Bracken Self-Selection Fabrics Limited*[82] identified the background precedent and the manner in which this will be applied by the Courts. In this case, the parties were in the midst of arbitration proceedings when the Landlord subsequently accepted two quarters of rent <u>after</u> the Lease was terminated by irritancy as a result of an unauthorised use of the premises by a Sub-tenant. Lord Coulsfield commented that "*I respectfully agree that acceptance of rent is, in all normal circumstances, an act so unequivocal that it must be taken to amount to a waiver of irritancy*"[83]. However, and whilst he commented that "*if the payment had been immediately returned, as was the first payment in September, I would have had little difficulty in reaching the view that......*

81 2009 CSIH 71

82 1990 SCLR 677

83 Page 683

the irritancy had not been waived"[84], he concluded in this case that the irritancy had not been waived due to the arbitration being commenced before the rent was accepted. It was, however, explained as a special set of circumstances, which, in my view, will not be mirrored in most instances. The onus of establishing the irritancy was not waived will not be a simple case of pleading it was an oversight, although, evidently, each case will be determined on its own merits, facts and circumstances.

In *Glasgow City Council V Morrison Developments Limited*[85] the Court held that an obligation to make payment of a grassum and to undertake certain works did not negatively prescribe[86] and the Landlords were justified in their endeavours to irritate the Lease as a result of the breaches in question.

---

[84] Page 682

[85] 2003 SCLR 276

[86] In terms of s6 of the Prescription and Limitation (Scotland) Act 1973

CHAPTER FOUR

IRRITANCY – NON-MONETARY BREACHES

Sections 5 of the Law Reform (Miscellaneous Provisions) (Scotland) Act 1985, similar to the application of section 4 in respect of monetary breaches, applies a benchmark protection for non-monetary breaches by Tenants in commercial leases. Again, it cannot be contracted out of.[87] It provides, under subsection (1), that a clause enabling a Landlord to terminate a Lease for (1) any non-monetary breach; (2) a matter that is considered, or expressly deemed to be, a material breach; and/or (3) a change of circumstances of the Tenant; cannot be exercised unless, in all the circumstances, the Landlord can demonstrate it has acted in a fair and reasonable manner in doing so. Subsection 3 goes on to set out that, in determining the nature of a breach that can still be remedied, it shall be taken into account whether a <u>reasonable opportunity</u> has been afforded to the Tenant to enable the breach to be rectified.

There are a handful of cases that elicit the manner in which Section 5 will be applied in the context of non-monetary breaches, including insolvency as a change of circumstances, justifying irritancy of a Lease. Typically, a well-drafted conventional irritancy clause will permit a Landlord to irritate the Lease in the event of a non-monetary breach as well as the appointment of a trustee in sequestration and, in the context of a Limited Company, the appointment of an administrator, receiver, liquidator of the Tenant or, more recently, the agreement of a Company Voluntary Arrangement, otherwise known as a CVA (all being matters incapable of being remedied in terms of the express wording of s5 of the 1985 Act). The Landlord may wish to terminate

[87] S6 of the 1985 Act

the Lease due to what it sees as a significant and material change in circumstances and financial standing of its original Tenant, whereas an insolvency practitioner will want to be given time to find a successor of the leasehold interest and business carried on at the premises.

Generally, and at the adjustment stage of the draft Lease itself, a balance is often struck where the irritancy clause will permit the insolvency practitioner typically between 6 and 12 months without incurring an irritancy to fulfil this remit. This is usually conditional upon the insolvency practitioner personally adopting liability for all of the Tenant's obligations under the Lease within a set time frame, commonly 21 days from appointment, and a failure to do so will usually then permit the Landlord to proceed with irritancy. Landlords should, however, note that, in the context of an administration of a Tenant Company, the Landlord cannot irritate the Lease unless it has either obtained: (a) the consent of the administrator; or (b) the permission of the Court.[88] Most commercial property advisers to Landlords will seek to terminate a Lease via irritancy on the more firm grounding of arrears of monetary sums under the Lease, which, as we have seen under s4, do not require a discussion on acting in a fair and reasonable manner as is required for non-monetary breaches under s5 of the 1985 Act.

In the case of *Auditglen Limited V SCOTEC Industries Limited*[89] a variation of the irritancy clause in a Lease within a subsequent assignation was held not to extend the Landlord's rights to irritate the Lease in the event of the receivership of the Tenant Company where there were original provisions for liquidation. It is a reminder that solicitors should not perceive a reference to other circumstances permitting irritancy to automatically extend to similar insolvency scenarios affecting a Limited Company at any one time. Express reference needs to

---

[88] Paragraph 43(5) of Schedule B1 of the Insolvency Act 1986 (as varied by the introduction of the Enterprise Act 2002)

[89] 1996 SLT 493

be the way to go if an irritancy is to be sought firmly on the grounds of a change of circumstances due to an insolvency event.

In *Aubrey Investments Limited V DSC (Realisations) Limited (in receivership)*[90] we were provided with a number of observations by Lord Macfadyen. Receivers were appointed for the Tenant Company on 3rd September 1996 and, following the failure of the receivers to accept responsibility under the Lease, the Landlords sought to irritate the Lease on 24th January 1997, with an abortive application for consent to assign the Lease also taking place between the dates in question. The Tenants were arguing that, in terms of s5 of the 1985 Act, a fair and reasonable Landlord would not have terminated the Lease. In what was a helpful and clear judgement, Lord Macfadyen, in finding in favour of the Landlords, set out that:

1. The level of knowledge of the Landlord is to be taken into context in determining whether the overall termination was fair and reasonable in all the circumstances, albeit a failure by the Landlord to make inquiries, when it is expected to do so, will also be taken into account;[91]

2. The onus of establishing that a fair and reasonable Landlord would not have terminated the Lease, in all the circumstances, is on the Tenant entity challenging the Landlord;[92]

3. The relevant time for considering whether the Landlord acted fairly and reasonably is the point at which the irritancy notice was served and not, for example, the date of the appointment of the receivers;[93]

---

90 1999 SC 21

91 Page 42

92 Page 43

93 Page 44

4. The fair and reasonable Landlord test, amongst many constituent elements, involves consideration of the losses likely to be suffered by both parties in determining whether the Lease is to be terminated or kept intact, but the test is not to be reduced to a simple balancing of hardship overall;[94]

5. The words "*fair and reasonable*" should not be split up and analysed separately, rather they are part of the one singular expression;[95]

6. Timing is important in the application of the fair and reasonable Landlord test. It is not a case of providing an insolvency practitioner with infinite time to dispose of the Lease, and it is inevitable that a fair and reasonable Landlord will decide, at some point, that sufficient opportunity has been given to the insolvency practitioner;[96] and

7. It is acceptable for a fair and reasonable Landlord to include its own commercial interest in its considerations. The mere fact that a certain course of action produces a collateral benefit to the Landlord does not, automatically, taint the action as unfair and/or unreasonable;[97]

The case of *Maris V Banchory Squash Racquets Club*[98] involved the application of s5 to a breach of the repairing obligation imposed on the Tenant in a Lease. The Lease required the Tenant to construct and thereafter maintain, within 5 years of its date of entry, squash courts and associated offices. Interestingly, the Lease did not have a conventional irritancy clause, but it did have a general clause permitting the

[94] Page 46

[95] Page 44

[96] Page 49

[97] Page 50

[98] 2007 SC 501

Landlord to terminate the contract in the event of a material breach by the Tenant. The case, therefore, affirmed that the criteria of s5 will apply irrespective of whether a lease is being irritated by conventional irritancy or as a result of a breach of contract (in the absence of an express irritancy clause). The Landlords were seeking to irritate the Lease following the failure of the Tenant to address various wants of repair within a 3 month period, and which were narrated within a Schedule of Dilapidations. The Tenants, during the 3 month period in question, only undertook 2 wants of repair, but had, by the end of the judicial proceedings for declarator and decree, undertaken far more repairs set out in the original Schedule. Lord Eassie affirmed the earlier comments in *Aubrey Investments*[99], namely that the question of the irritancy decision being taken by a fair and reasonable Landlord was at the point of the Notice of Irritancy being served and not thereafter, and he found in favour of the Landlord in this instance.

The case of *Crieff Highland Gathering Limited V Perth and Kinross Council*[100] involved another instance where there was no irritancy clause in the Lease. As such, the Landlords sought to terminate the Lease on the basis of a material breach arising from the failure of the Tenant to address repairs within a specified 3 month period. The Tenants argued that the Landlord did not act fairly and reasonably in all the circumstances as required by s5 of the 1985 Act. In finding in favour of the Tenant overall, the court held that, whilst the Tenant was in breach of its repairing obligation, and did not undertake the wants of repair timeously, the breach was not material in its nature to justify rescission of the contract under s5.

Lord Pentland opined that the breach of the repairing obligation was not material because full and uninterrupted use of the premises was continuing throughout, and the wants of repair, predominantly

---

[99] See citation at 4

[100] 2011 CSOH 78

pertaining to boundary walls, were not of "*such fundamental gravity as to touch on the very essence of the contract.*"[101] There was no attempt to exercise the Landlord's express rights to step in and carry out the works and seek recovery of the expense in doing so, nor to seek an order of specific implement to ordain the Tenant to undertake the works. Lord Pentland also commented that the tenant's future intentions to remain in possession during the proof were important because "*the courts have traditionally been reluctant to allow a rural lease without an irritancy clause to be bought to an end in circumstances where the Tenant has made it clear that it intends to perform its side of the contract during the remaining period of the Lease.*"[102] As such, Lord Pentland made it clear that, for a lease to be rescinded, there must be a material breach, there must be a fair and reasonable opportunity to fulfil the Tenant's contractual obligations (and in this instance he felt 3 months were insufficient to undertake the wants of repair due to the winter climate) and, lastly, it must be demonstrated that the Tenant is unwilling or unable to perform in the future.[103] Lastly, Lord Pentland opined that "*it would not be fair and reasonable [in terms of s5 of the 1985 Act].... to opt for termination where there are alternative remedies available which would (a) not deprive the tenant of its interest in the lease but (b) nevertheless adequately protect the landlord's interest.*"[104] As such, we can see that the test imposed by s5 for material breaches in a lease, without a conventional irritancy clause, will require other options to be explored, and possibly exhausted, before the courts will uphold an instance of rescission of the lease due to material breach of contract.

Lastly, on the theme of termination of a Lease, it has been held in the case of *ELB Securities Limited V Love*[105] that, upon a Company being

---

[101] Paragraph 45

[102] Paragraph 46

[103] Paragraph 54

[104] Paragraph 58

[105] 2015 CSIH 67

dissolved and struck off Companies House, the Tenant's interest at that point passes to the Crown as *bona vacantia*[106] and, upon the Crown issuing a disclaimer on 15th June 2013, the rights in the Lease were ended indefinitely. Lady Paton commented that certainty was a very important factor, from a Landlord's perspective, and, as such, a Landlord could not be expected to see if the Company was restored to an "*as you were*" position in the 6-year period flowing from it being dissolved. It is therefore very important for Tenants to ensure that they address the administrative requirements of Companies House timeously in order to avoid losing leasehold interests unnecessarily.

[106] S1012 of the Companies Act 2006

CHAPTER FIVE

THE IMPACT OF *CONFUSIO*

The principle of *confusio* in Scots Law can be traced back to Roman Law and, at its most basic level, provides that a debtor and creditor cannot be the same party in a contract. In this chapter I will predominantly concentrate on the application of *confusio* to commercial leases. It is often suggested that *confusio* relates to the merging of debtor and creditor obligations into the name of one party as personal rights, whereas *consolidatio* relates to the similar merging of real rights rather than personal rights into the same party. This is, and to some degree remains, an active and ongoing academic discussion and, for the purposes of this chapter, we will concentrate on *confusio* overall, particularly given that the most recent decision on this note in the House of Lords, *Clydesdale Bank V Davidson,*[107] does not make such a distinction, and it was not held that the rental obligation alone would be suspended or that the Lease would continue to subsist in any shape or form.[108]

One of the earliest instances of the application of *confusio* can be traced back to the 1867 case of *Campbell V McKinnon,*[109] where an acquisition of the feudal charter by a tenant under the existing lease was held to extinguish the lease. Professor MacDonald also confirmed his agreement to the application of *confusio* to this situation by summarising that "*the better view is that confusio does operate absolutely to extinguish the lease itself.....*"[110]. Similarly, in *Lord Blantyre V Dunn*[111], where the

[107] 1998 SC (HL) 51

[108] See Clydesdale Bank plc V Davidson commentary at Chapter 1

[109] 1867 5 M 636

[110] Professor MacDonald's Conveyancing Opinions (1998) at page 201

[111] 1858 20 D 1188

tenant acquired the land originally subject to a lease, Lord Mackenzie commented that "*the tenant had become the proprietor..... He was the sole party liable for the rents, if any rent was due. But he himself was simply and absolutely creditor in the obligation for rent, as well as debtor in that same obligation. Of necessity, confusio took effect, there being nothing done to prevent it, the whole obligations under the Lease were therefore gone.*"[112]

Chapter 1 of this book comments on the cases of *Pinkerton V Pinkerton*[113] and *Clydesdale Bank plc V Davidson* in the context of Landlord and Tenant needing to be separate and distinct parties, and, as such, both decisions will not be repeated hereunder. It is noted that the latter, being a House of Lords decision, determined that the lesser of the 2 competing interests in a property would effectively be trumped by the greater right and could not subsist together. The decision in *Clydesdale Bank Plc V Davidson* was subsequently applied in *Serup V McCormack*,[114] where a lease was held to have been extinguished by *confusio* following the transfer of the heritable interest to the original tenant and another party in pro-indiviso shares.

A question that often crops up in practice is whether a Sublease can continue to subsist where the Head Lease is extinguished by *confusio* as a result of the Head Tenant (or Mid-Landlord) subsequently acquiring ownership of the premises. An early opinion of Professor Halliday was used to confirm a sublease would continue to subsist under these circumstances in the case of *Howgate Shopping Centre Limited V Catercraft Services Limited.*[115] Lord Macfadyen commented that "*in my opinion the amalgamation of the landlord's and tenant's interest in the lease had no effect on the subsistence of the Sublease. That question*

[112] Page 1197

[113] 1986 SLT 672

[114] 2012 SCLR 189

[115] 2004 SCLR 739

relating to the position of the Subtenant when the interest of the Landlord in the sublease and the interest of the Landlord in lease come into the same hands appears to have been addressed directly only by Professor Halliday (Conveyancing Opinions, p380) who said "it makes no sense that valid subleases or heritable securities created over registered leases can be extinguished by the lessee acquiring the property, a transaction to which neither the subtenants nor the heritable creditors are parties". I agree with that view".[116] As such, the Sublease was held to have remained fully intact, despite effectively imposing the same obligations set out in the original Head Lease.

[116] Paragraph 60

CHAPTER SIX

RENUNCIATION

A renunciation is an agreement, entered into between a Landlord and a Tenant, to voluntarily terminate a Lease in advance of its natural expiry date. As with any contract, it is important to ensure that all terms are agreed and reduced to writing, so that the parties are clear in their respective obligations, if any, both in the run-up to, on and and indeed after the date of legal surrender. The purpose of this chapter is simply to summarise the relevant considerations to be borne in mind when finalising a renunciation of a Lease for a Landlord or a Tenant.

(a) The Parties

In addition to both Landlord and Tenant, the renunciation should effectively introduce any guarantor so that the obligation on the guarantor to perform any of the Tenant's obligations is discharged simultaneously, albeit this could be achieved by a separate discharge by the Landlord if easier. If there is a standard security over the heritable interest then it is highly likely that the consent of the lender should be sought, although the terms and conditions of the original lending facility will need to be checked carefully. If there is a standard security over the tenant's long leasehold interest then the lender will need to grant a discharge in order to completely close off the long leasehold title sheet in the Land Register of Scotland when the registration of the signed renunciation is submitted to Registers of Scotland.

(b) Scope of Obligations being Terminated

A renunciation will normally terminate all obligations, whether monetary or non-monetary, and whether past, present and future, with effect from a certain date. As such, it is essential that any obligations that are yet to be performed or addressed are excluded from the ambit of the renunciation. A failure to exclude these obligations, for example a dilapidations claim, or an apportionment of rent, service charges and insurance premia, will result in no such performance being legally enforceable upon the termination of the Lease.

(c) Payment of a Premium

It is quite often the case that a payment will be made on the termination date of a renunciation. In general terms, a premium moving from the Tenant to the Landlord is classed as a reverse premium. As such, it is wholly outside of the scope of Land and Buildings Transaction Tax[117], otherwise known as LBTT, no matter what the amount in question actually is. If the premium is, however, moving from Landlord to Tenant then it will be subject to the realms of notification by the Landlord and, if necessary, payment of the relevant amount of tax, in terms of the thresholds set by Revenue Scotland, in accordance with the 2013 Act, at the effective date in question.

The VAT position of the relevant party receiving the sum of money also needs to be carefully considered. If the party in question has waived its exemption to VAT, otherwise known as opting to tax the property in question, then VAT will be payable on the payment of the premium, in exchange for a VAT invoice. However, if the payment is being made by the Tenant and is effectively in lieu of accrued dilapidations, which will not be undertaken by the Tenant, then VAT is not

[117] Paragraph 14 of Part 5 of Schedule 19 of the Land and Buildings Transaction Tax (Scotland) Act 2013

chargeable on that element of the premium. It should also be borne in mind that the calculation of LBTT on a premium should always be inclusive of any element of VAT payable on the payment. If the original Lease was notifiable to Revenue Scotland, following the introduction of LBTT in Scotland in April 2015, then a further LBTT Return will need to be submitted by the Tenant's agent in order to intimate the termination of the Lease and to ensure that there is no need to submit 3-yearly returns after the date of surrender.

(d) Impact on Pre-Existing Sublease

An interesting question arises as to the status of a Sublease where the Head Landlord and Head Tenant have agreed to, and subsequently entered into, a renunciation of the Head Lease. Whilst we have considered the impact of *confusio* in chapter 5, it is not entirely clear that the sublease will be treated as remaining alive, given there is no direct contractual relationship between the Head Landlord and the Sub-Tenant. If it is understood that the Head Landlord will expect vacant possession from the Head Tenant, under the terms of the renunciation, and a failure to return vacant possession will be a breach of the grant of the warrandice clause in the renunciation itself, then the Head Tenant would be wisely advised to ensure that a separate renunciation is entered into with the Sub-Tenant. A failure to do so could produce the very unsatisfactory position of the Head Landlord claiming a breach of warrandice against the Head Tenant, and the Sub-Tenant, in turn, claiming a breach of warrandice by the Head Tenant arising from the renunciation of the Head Lease coming after the grant of warrandice in the Sublease itself. If the objective of the whole exercise is for the Head Tenant to leave, and for the Subtenant to remain in possession of the property, then one would suggest that an assignation of the Head Lease by the Head Tenant to the Subtenant, or a renunciation of the Head Lease coupled with a simultaneous grant of a new Lease directly by the Head Landlord to the Subtenant, would be the safest and most pragmatic solution for all parties involved.

CHAPTER SEVEN

REI INTERITUS

Most practitioners will expect commercial leases to expressly provide that they will not be terminated in the event of damage or destruction of all or part of the property. Such a clause will usually go on and provide the Landlord with a period of 3 years to reconstruct or reinstate the premises, assuming any buildings insurance has not been vitiated by the actions of the Tenant. The rent and other pecuniary payments payable by the Tenant will usually be suspended, in whole or in part, depending on the extent of the damage, until the property is reinstated. In the event that the reinstatement is not completed by the 3rd anniversary of the damage or destruction taking place then both parties would usually be entitled, but not bound, to terminate the Lease. The reason for this is to prevent the application of the common law principle of *rei interitus*. In the absence of express wording to the contrary, *rei interitus* would apply to terminate a Lease in the event of any damage, destruction or other issues prohibiting possession and use of the premises by the Tenant. The damage, destruction or other factor(s) must not be directly caused by the Tenant.

One of the very earliest of decisions, *Duff V Fleming*,[118] emphasised the application of *rei interitus* at its most basic level. It was held that a repairing obligation imposed upon a Tenant in a Lease to keep the premises in good order and repair did not extend to imposing legal responsibility for total damage and/or destruction. The Landlord's action for rental, following the premises being vacated by the Tenant, was unsuccessful. Lord Cowan commented that "*of the general principle that the destruction of the subject for the purpose for which it was let,*

[118] 1870 8 M 769

by accidental fire or from other fortuitous event, puts an end to the contract of lease, there can be no doubt."[119]

It was also made clear that partial damage or destruction may not be sufficient to terminate the Lease if the premises occupied by a Tenant remain fit for their intended use and the purposes for which they were originally let. This decision was re-affirmed in *Cantors Properties (Scotland) Limited V Swears & Wells Limited,*[120] where Lord Cameron emphasised that parties are free to agree anything to the contrary, namely "*If parties wish to keep a contract of lease alive, even if during the stipulated currency of the Lease the physical subject may be destroyed, it is within their legal competence to do so. There is nothing in the authorities in the law of Scotland which forbids this exercise of the right of freedom of contract."*[121]

The specific question of partial damage and destruction was explored, in greater detail, in the case of *James Allan V James Markland.*[122] In this case, a shoe shop was damaged by fire and the Tenant sought to return the keys and possession back to the Landlord as a result of the damage. Evidence was led that the damage was solely to the rear store room premises and that the repairs, other than painting, could have been completed in 5 days. Lord Shand held that the lease did not terminate under *rei interitus*, commenting that "*the destruction of a part of the subject of the lease will not release the tenant, unless the part be essential for the purpose for which the premises were let; and in determining the question whether the subject was either or in a material part so destroyed as to make it unfit for the purposes for which it was let, a case of destruction is not made out by showing that the premises have been made uncomfortable and, I would add, unsuitable for the purpose of the lease*

[119] Page 771

[120] 1978 SC 310

[121] Page 315

[122] 1882 10 R 383

for a short time. The question whether the premises have been made unfit for the purpose of the tenant's occupation is one of degree."[123] Lord Mure also summarised, rather succinctly, in the same case, that "*If the business could without any considerable inconvenience be carried on during the repairs, and these repairs could have been made within a reasonable time, the tenant must still be held bound by his Lease.*"[124]

Whilst the above cases have involved physical damage and destruction, the case of *The Tay Salmon Fisheries Company Limited V Alexander Speedie*[125] demonstrated that *rei interitus* is not necessarily restricted to such circumstances. In this case, the Tenant, a fishery company, was unable to use the leased premises for salmon fishing purposes because the President of the Air Council introduced a bye-law designating the majority of the leased premises as an area for aerial gunning and bombing practice. The area was designated, as such, for 4 days a week, and it was made illegal for anyone to access the area on these days. It was shown, in evidence, to be impractical and expensive for fishing nets to be deployed and then removed on the remaining 3 days of the week where the waters were not being used for their new bye-law status. Lord Sands commented that "*I have come ultimately to the conclusion that, even though the Air Ministry endeavour to exercise their rights civiliter, the value of the salmon fishings is destroyed, and that the area not affected is so small and of so little value that, if it is regarded as alone freely available, the character of the fishery is entirely altered.*"[126] This decision was also similarly applied in *Mackeson V Boyd*[127] to hold that the tenant of a furnished mansion house and lands, which were requisitioned by the military during the war, was tantamount to constructive total

123 Page 389

124 Page 393

125 1929 SC 593

126 Pages 603 and 604

127 1942 SC 56

eviction, which was sufficient to deprive the tenant of the use of the majority of the property, and the lease was held to be at an end.

In *Robert Purvis Plant Hire Limited V Brewster*[128] the court refused to apply *rei interitus* to a set of circumstances where an enforcement notice was served by Edinburgh Council on a tenant in a commercial lease. The enforcement notice was alleging a breach of planning laws following the use of the premises by the tenant for the recycling of construction and demolition materials. It required the Tenant to cease such use and remove such offending materials from the site within 2 months of its service. The Court noted that the tenant was under an express obligation to comply with planning laws under the terms of the Lease and, in accepting this obligation, the Tenant was compelled, at its own risk and expense, to obtain whatever planning consent was needed to continue with its proposed use of the premises. There was no question of any liability resting with the Landlord, in view of the express wording adjusted and agreed between the parties to the contrary.

[128] 2009 Hous LR 34

CHAPTER EIGHT

TACIT RELOCATION AND STATUTORY RENEWAL

(A) Tacit Relocation

The principle of tacit relocation, in leases, is inherited in Scotland from Roman Law. In the absence of a notice to quit being served, at least 40 clear days prior to natural expiry, Scots Law assumes both Landlord and Tenant wish the Lease to continue, on the same terms and conditions, by default. The Lease shall continue for the lower period of (a) one year; and (b) the original term of the Lease. Lord Watson summarised in *Neilson V Mossend Iron Co*[129] that "*the legal effect of tacit relocation is that all the stipulations and conditions of the original contract remain in force, in so far as they are not inconsistent with any implied term of the renewed contract.*"[130]

We can glean a number of important points from the leading cases in this area. The case of *MacDougall V Guidi*[131] is continuing authority for the proposition that common law obligations can be contracted out of by express agreement, and this case expressly referred to tacit relocation. In such circumstances, if there is express wording to exclude tacit relocation at the outset of the lease, no notice whatsoever requires to be given prior to the natural expiry date in order to terminate the Lease.

---

129 1886 13 R (HL) 50

130 Page 54

131 1992 SCLR 167

In *Smith V Grayton Estates Limited*[132] the court held that a notice to quit, served by one of two tenants in a joint agricultural tenancy, was sufficient to terminate the Lease at its natural expiry and prohibit the continuation by tacit relocation. Lord President Clyde commented that "*In the case of tacit relocation the law implies consent if all the parties are silent on the matter. Hence where there are joint tenants, tacit consent by both of them is necessary to secure the prolongation and to enable tacit relocation to operate. Silence by both is necessary to presume that both the tenants wish the tenancy to continue for another year. On the other hand, if both are not silent, and if one gives due notice of termination, the consent necessary for tacit relocation to operate is demonstrably not present and tacit relocation will not operate beyond the date of termination in the notice. Clearly in the present case, there is no such tacit consent and, in my view, a notice by one of the two joint tenants is enough to exclude the further operation of tacit relocation.*"[133]

The case of *Signet Group Plc V C & J Clark Retail Properties Limited*[134] was an important case in affirming the background approach pertaining to two separate points. The Tenant sought to resist the Lease continuing for another year, and argued that a faxed notice dated 5th April 1993 should be deemed sufficient for a termination date of 15th May later that year – being the 40th day – from the date of faxing. It was also argued that the Tenant's physical removal from the property in February of that same year should, in any event, overcome the need for a formal notice completely. Firstly, Lord Weir emphasised that "*the law has long been settled that 40 clear days' notice is required so as to prevent the operation of tacit relocation in a Lease. It has never before been questioned that anything less will suffice in this field of law and in the absence of authority to the contrary we consider that it is too late now to*

132 1960 SC 349

133 Pages 354 and 355

134 1996 SC 444

seek to challenge the long-established custom."[135] As such, the Tenant did not exclude the operation of tacit relocation timeously, and the Court did not need to go on and comment on whether service by fax was sufficient or not. In terms of the other argument, Lord Weir also made it clear that "*it is very difficult to envisage a case where any actings short of some form of notice, whether communicated verbally or in writing, would ever suffice.*"[136] Accordingly, it was held that the Lease had, in fact, continued under tacit relocation.

Similar to discussions in other chapters, it is possible for subsequent conduct, namely after the service of a notice to quit, to be tantamount to deem the Lease to continue by tacit relocation beyond the natural expiry date. In *Milner's Curator Bonis V Mason,*[137] a Landlord continued to accept the payment of rent, without qualification, for a period of 6 months after serving a notice to quit. Sheriff Substitute Cormack Cohen commented that "*in my opinion there is a clear presumption, entirely unrebutted by averment, that the landlord in unreservedly accepting rent had departed from the notice to quit.*"[138] And, similarly, in *Coatbridge Town Council V Tamburrino*[139] it was held by Sheriff-substitute Thomas Young that "*at common law a Landlord who has served a notice to quit and who thereafter accepts rent is held to have departed from the notice to quit and to have lost his right to regain possession of the subject of lease as at that term.*"[140]

There have also been some cases on the actual terms upon which tacit relocation has continued a lease beyond its natural expiry date. In *The*

[135] Page 448

[136] Page 447

[137] 1965 SLT (Sh Ct) 56

[138] Page 57

[139] 1958 SLT (Sh Ct) 4

[140] Page 5

Commercial Union Assurance Company Limited V Watt & Cumine[141] the tenants were party to a lease that had an option to extend, and only after the lease had continued by operation of tacit relocation did they wish to exercise their option to extend by a period longer than the automatic one year period. It was held by Lord President Clyde that "*one of these implied terms [of tacit relocation] is that during tacit relocation either party may terminate the lease by the requisite notice at the end of a year. It necessarily follows, in my view, from this that an option to the tenant to demand a further 20 years' lease is quite inconsistent with the landlord's rights under a lease from year to year. It appears to me that once the stipulated duration of the lease had expired and they had become yearly tenancies, the right to exercise the option had flown off.*"[142] And in *Sea Breeze Properties Limited V Bio-Medical Systems Limited*[143] an option that was specified to be exercised on one occasion, to either extend the Lease or purchase the premises at market value, had already been exercised prior to the continuation of the Lease under tacit relocation. Furthermore, it was held to be one occasion only and not once in any subsequent year as was argued by the Landlords. And in *Allied Dunbar Assurance Plc V Superglass Sections Limited*[144] a Landlord argued that a Tenant's notice to quit, served prior to natural expiry, in circumstances where it was in breach of its repairing obligation, should be invalid. The basis put forward, namely that the breach of the repairing obligation was contrary to the mutuality of contractual obligations, was, unsurprisingly, unsuccessful. The Landlord had a separate remedy for any breach of contract, and it was in no way linked to the termination of the Lease, and the notice to quit ensuring tacit relocation did not apply was upheld.

---

[141] 1964 SC 84

[142] Page 88

[143] 1998 SLT 319

[144] 2003 SLT 1420

Avoiding Decree for Possession After Natural Expiry

Sections 34 to 37 of the Sheriff Courts (Scotland) Act 1907 narrate circumstances in which judicial proceedings may not be required in order to recover possession of a premises following the termination of a Lease. The provisions in question are notorious for being difficult to interpret, and my own personal favourite summary is by Messrs Gretton and Reid, who opine that "*those who have studied ss 34 to 37 of the Sheriff Courts (Scotland) Act 1907 are few. Fewer still are those who have studied these provisions and emerged both alive and sane.*"[145]

In summary, s34 provides that a premises in excess of 2 acres in extent, under a probative lease, can be terminated, and possession recovered with the Extract alone as if it was a decree of removal, if the Landlord serves notice to the Tenant. The period of the notice is dependent on the duration of the Lease. A lease in excess of 3 years necessitates notice of at least a year and not more than two years[146]. Leases of a duration that are less than 3 years, including those continuing on a yearly rolling basis by tacit relocation or otherwise, necessitate notice of at least 6 months[147]. The provision goes on to specify that a failure to comply with the provision will ensure the lease continues for another year by tacit relocation, and that the procedure is only valid within 6 weeks of the natural expiry date. In *Lormor Limited V Glasgow City Council*[148] the Landlord argued that the Act required the Tenant of a premises exceeding 2 acres in extent to give at least 6 months of notice, mirroring the timeframe set out for the Landlords. In failing to do so, the argument was that it resulted in the Lease continuing for another year under tacit relocation. Lord Menzies found in favour of the Tenant, namely that 40 days of notice was sufficient to terminate the Lease,

[145] Conveyancing 2019 at Page 114

[146] Section 34(A) of the 1907 Act

[147] Section 34(B) of the 1907 Act

[148] 2014 SC 213

He commented that "*Section 34 is directed at the situation in which the Landlord initiates termination and wishes to utilise the new remedy created by the section [to avoid the necessity of a decree for removal after the date of natural expiry]. We see no justification for reading into these provisions a requirement that in the different situation of a tenant who wishes to initiate a termination there is a requirement to give the same period of notice….. If Parliament had intended to introduce a requirement to give not less than six months' notice of termination both on the Landlord and on the Tenant, it could easily have done so. That it did not do so is telling. We consider that not less than 40 days' notice of termination by a Tenant will suffice to prevent tacit relocation. In this regard, we do not consider that s34 of the 1907 Act has innovated on the requirements of the common law.*"[149] And in the subsequent recent case of *M7 Real Estate Investments Partners VI Industrial Propco Limited V Amazon UK Services Limited,*[150] the court followed the decision in *Lormor.* In that case a Landlord of premises exceeding 2 acres, for an original duration of 15 years, served a Notice to Quit, providing notice of more than 40 days but less than 6 months, in advance of the termination date. The Tenant argued that the Lease had continued by tacit relocation as a result of the Landlord's failure to comply with the timescale set out in s 34. Lord Ericht held that the lease had indeed terminated and the Notice to Quit was clearly sufficient to prohibit tacit relocation applying. In his judgement he commented that s34 was to be perceived as an expedited procedure for recovering possession of a property without decree. Furthermore, he commented that "*the proviso does not make a substantive change to the law on tacit relocation. It is not a free-standing provision independent of the procedure for removal without an action for removing introduced by s 34. It applies only when that procedure is used.*"[151] In other words, a Notice to Quit, at least 40 clear days, served by either party on the other, will be sufficient to prohibit tacit

[149] Paragraphs 22 and 23

[150] 2020 SCLR 370

[151] Paragraph 15

relocation, and the s34 procedure requiring longer periods of notice is only where the Landlord wishes to avoid having to obtain a court decree for possession if the Tenant does not vacate timeously.

(B) Statutory Protection Afforded to Shops at Natural Expiry

The Tenancy of Shops (Scotland) Act 1949, as continued and varied by the Tenancy of Shops (Scotland) Act 1964, provides a statutory renewal regime for tenants coming to the end of their tenure of a Lease. Section 1 of the Act provides that a Tenant that is provided with a Notice to Quit from its Landlord, and is unable to agree a renewal, may apply to a Sheriff Court within 21 days of the receipt of the Notice to Quit for a renewal. Under Subsection (2), a Sheriff has the power to renew the lease for a maximum period of one year and, otherwise, on terms and conditions deemed reasonable by the Sheriff. The provision makes it clear that such term shall be deemed to be a new lease rather than a continuation.

Subsection (3) provides the Sheriff with the power to dismiss the application if:

- The tenant is in breach of the lease, in a material sense, in the Sheriff's opinion;

- The tenant is bankrupt or, if a Company, is otherwise unable to pay its debts;

- The Landlord has offered to sell the premises to the Tenant at an agreed price, failing which the price can be determined by a single arbiter, failing which the Sheriff;

- The Landlord has offered the Tenant alternative suitable premises to the Tenant;

- The Landlord has contracted to let, sell or otherwise taken steps following the service of a notice to quit by the Tenant, and a renewal would now cause the Landlord prejudice if vacant possession was not obtained from the Tenant;

- In all the circumstances, there would be greater hardship in continuing the lease instead of permitting it to terminate.

Subsection (4) provides that the statutory renewal procedure can be utilised by a Tenant more than once for the same property and Landlord.

A few of the cases citing the Acts have given us an insight into how the legislation will be applied by the Courts. In *Golder V Thomas Johnston's (Bakers) Limited*[152] a blacksmith was refused protection under the Acts by the Court. Sheriff Substitute Dewar Gibb commented that "*I think the Act here is pointing exclusively to a place where goods are kept (not made) and sold by a dealer or merchant (who is not the same as a manufacturer). This is quite different from what the applicant does. The applicant supplies wholesalers to order and occasionally supplies an odd retail buyer. Making all allowance for the wide sense of shops given by the Acts, all the facts here seem to preclude me from holding this to be a shop and I must dismiss the application.*"[153] The case of *Craig V Saunders & Connor Limited*[154] demonstrated that a premises occupied by an optician would be classed as a shop and that, overall, whilst there would be hardship to both parties in whatever outcome was determined, it was felt necessary, on balance, to give the tenant a renewal of 6 months at a higher rent. In *Ashley Wallpaper Company Limited V Morrisons Associated Companies Limited*[155] it was determined that the statutory

---

[152] 1950 SLT (Sh Ct) 50

[153] Page 51

[154] 1962 SLT (Sh Ct) 85

[155] 1952 SLT (Sh Ct) 25

protection afforded to Tenants under the Acts would not extend to any Subtenants of shop premises. In *Robertson V Bass Holdings*[156] the Landlord served a notice to quit on the tenant of licensed premises in Edinburgh. The two alternative premises offered by the Landlord was not considered to be reasonable alternative accommodation and, accordingly, the lease was renewed for another year. In *Superdrug Stores Plc V Network Rail Infrastructure Limited*[157] it was determined that an application under the Act was lodged on the day that a procedurally valid summons was lodged with the Sheriff Court and not, for example, the date of processing or validation thereafter. This was critical to the application as it was lodged on the 21st day from the Notice to Quit and would not have been valid thereafter. In the case of *Edinburgh Woollen Mill Limited V Singh*[158] Sheriff Ross went out of his way to look at the reasoning behind the Acts in then seeking to apply the contents to this situation. He commented that "*the mischief which the 1949 Act was designed to address is no longer evident today, but I have no doubt that in 1949 it was sufficiently notorious not to require spelling out. Small scale traders were being unfairly treated and forced out of business by unscrupulous property speculators, who saw an opportunity for profit at the expense of community welfare........ The 1949 Act does not empower the court to act as a planning authority, or to regulate competition between businesses.... Turning to the present case, it is at once apparent that no such considerations exist. The pursuer's business [cited earlier in the case as being a turnover of £161m and profit after tax if £19m] will be somewhat diminished by ceasing trade from the premises, but otherwise continues uninterrupted from its 300 other outlets. There is no threat to its goodwill or good name, as it can adapt other stores to carry their name, if they wish. The present dispute represents no more than an attempt to retain a highly successful site, and to keep it from a direct competitor..... It is not an injustice, and there is nothing unreasonable in*

[156] 1993 SLT (Sh Ct) 55

[157] 2006 SC 365

[158] 2013 SLT (Sh Ct) 141

requiring the pursuer to remove at the end of the Lease."[159] These comments should, however, be contrasted to those made in *Select Service Partner Limited V Network Rail Limited.*[160] Sheriff Morrison held that the tenant only needed to start a discussion with Landlord before turning to seek the protection offered by the Acts. In dismissing the action by the Tenant, however, by applying the criteria set out in the Acts, he commented that he did not agree with Sheriff Ross's comments on the scope of the Acts in the *Edinburgh Woollen Mill Limited* case. He opined that "*There is, therefore, no legitimate ground in this case for looking at parliamentary material or otherwise in trying to construe the s.1(3) of the 1949 Act. The suggestion, on the other hand, that its application is restricted to applications by small shopkeepers against speculators or to avoid injustice, in the historic context of widespread economic oppression of small-scale shop traders, involves ambiguous language. How does one define a small shopkeeper or a speculator? If Parliament had intended to restrict the Act to small shopkeepers, it could easily have said so....... In summary, in my opinion, the 1949 Act, and s1 in particular, is clear, unambiguous, not obscure and does not lead to absurd results. It is not permissible to look at outside aids to construe.*"[161] He did, however, go on to comment that "*it may be more difficult for a multi-million pound company than a small shopkeeper to rely on some circumstances such as hardship justifying renewal of a tenancy.*"[162] It is clear that each application is determined on its merits, and, irrespective of the view of the purpose behind the Acts, we can see that the courts will consider the overall economic financial standing of the applicant and not just the profits accrued at the premises itself.

[159] Paragraphs 27 to 31

[160] 2015 SCLR 601

[161] Paragraphs 13 and 18

[162] Paragraph 19

CHAPTER NINE

A BRIEF ANALYSIS OF PROPOSALS FOR REFORM

Property law in Scotland has arguably seen more change in the last two decades than in the preceding 50-year period beforehand. For example, we kissed goodbye to the feudal system under The Abolition of Feudal Tenure (Scotland) Act 2000. We also codified the common law of title conditions and streamlined how they could be created, going forward, under the Title Conditions (Scotland) Act 2003 and the Tenement (Scotland) Act 2004. In particular, the concept of dual registration is worthy of praise alone and the legislation has added much clarity to an otherwise difficult area to apply in practice. The introduction of the Land Registration (Scotland) Act 2012 was welcomed for the concept of advance notices, eliminating the traditional gap between settlement and registration of title. Throughout all of this, however, the world of commercial leasing has been virtually unchanged, nonetheless adapting well, as required, to difficult market / trading conditions in the recession after 2008. And that, of course, is expected, given it is like any other contract to be negotiated and will depend, considerably, on the bargaining position of both parties. I say this with the exception of the Long Leases (Scotland) Act 2012, which introduced a welcome mechanism to convert many long leasehold chains into a heritable title upon an application to the Keeper.

In May 2018, the Scottish Law Commission launched its discussion paper on the reform of 6 aspects of commercial leasing, and invited responses for consideration by September of that same year. The reforms principally relate to termination, and the purpose of this chapter is to identify the broad aspects and to set out my own views on the extent of such reforms.

The First Aspect of Termination – Tacit Relocation

The principle of tacit relocation in leases is inherited in Scotland from Roman Law. As we have seen, in the absence of a notice to quit being served at least 40 days prior to natural expiry, Scots Law assumes both Landlord and Tenant wish the Lease to continue by default to the shorter of (a) one year; and (b) the original term of the Lease. Whilst this is a well-entrenched and recognised principle of Scots law, it is fair to say it is not always appreciated by clients. Every year I have at least two dozen clients – predominantly based down south – who are horrified to be told their Lease will continue notwithstanding their desire to return keys to the Landlord at lease expiry. This is solely down to a failure to serve a formal Notice to Quit.

The discussion paper explores whether tacit relocation should be disapplied completely, leaving contracting parties free to bring it in by express terms, and with the possibility of a statutory default regime if the Tenant remains in possession after natural expiry. The second option is that the law is clarified to state that tacit relocation can be contracted out of, possibly with it reviving if the parties find themselves continuing beyond Lease expiry.

My own view is that there is nothing to stop a Landlord and Tenant setting out a fixed term at the outset, and specifying the contract will continue on a monthly or yearly rolling basis thereafter, if no notice to quit is served. Accordingly, it would be my view that Scots law should set out the possibility of contracting out of tacit relocation (which I personally have always considered is possible to date). This can then be taken into account in the preparation of the Lease. The question of continuing possession beyond lease expiry is far trickier and should depend on the circumstances of the 4 essential elements of a Lease – parties, rent, duration and property – so if the same payment is continuing and accepted by the Landlord then I would favour an assumed 12 month rolling continuation until terminated by either party prior to the anniversary of the original expiry date.

The second aspect of termination – Notices to Quit

The discussion paper considers if there is any benefit in creating a statutory format for a Notice to Quit, and irrespective of whether it is served by a Tenant on the Landlord or vice versa. If not, the next consideration is whether there should be a set of essential elements that must be covered in any purported Notice to Quit. For example, some suggestions include the name of the party giving the notice, description of the let premises, date of termination, the serving party's notification to terminate, and, if notice is served by an agent, the details of the principal behind same. These are all essential elements that I believe are covered in any notice served by most, if not all, legal practitioners, but the difficulties tend to arise with unrepresented parties attempting to serve notices themselves. The other element that the discussion paper explores is the period of notice required, and whether 40 days is sufficient, irrespective of the duration of the term. There is a suggestion that 40 days in the modern era, given the complexities of dilapidations and the extent of tenant fit-out removal works required, may no longer represent sufficient time, and a comparison is made to break options, which typically require 6 months of notice. A break option, however, may be distinguished in that it is generally served by a Tenant to a Landlord to warn of a surrender in advance of lease expiry, and the bulk of the notice duration is to enable the Landlord to consider dilapidations and remarketing rather than return of vacant possession alone.

My own personal view is that the content of notices should prescribe essential elements to eradicate ambiguity. I would leave the parties to contract out of the default period of notice required for termination at natural expiry, and this would fit well with the concept of contracting out of tacit relocation (meaning no notice would be required, at all, in such circumstances). I remain open to the default 40 days being extended to, say, 2 months, prior to natural expiry, however I would wish the notice required for a break option to be as much or indeed as little as the parties have agreed in the Lease. For simplicity and transparency, I would not distinguish the period of notice required to take account of the length of term of the Lease, as is the case with the Private Residential Tenancies introduced by the Scottish Government in place of Assured Tenancies.

The third aspect of Termination – Apportionment of Rent

As we have seen, the English case of Marks and Spencer Plc V BNP Paribas Securities Services Trust Co (Jersey) Limited and another set a bit of a hare running for those of us in Scotland. It held that a Tenant that validly exercised its break option in a commercial Lease did not have the right to seek reimbursement of rent paid in advance attributable beyond the break date. As such, in England, the entitlement to recover rent in advance, paid beyond the break date, requires express wording in the Lease itself. The suggestions in many quarters are that the position is the same in Scotland and, personally, I have always held the view that a Tenant electing to terminate a Lease at a break date must have express wording necessitating a reimbursement of rent and, otherwise, is deemed to have offset advance rent already paid against the opportunity to escape for the exit earlier than expected. Invariably, in practice, the question will only arise in break options conditional upon all payments being up to date, as otherwise Tenants will simply pay up to the break date and leave Landlords to determine whether to pursue for other payments as well as any other antecedent breaches. The discussion paper considers whether the Apportionment Act 1870 should be amended to clarify the position, and my view remains that the position is sufficiently clear enough to avoid further legislation.

The Fourth Aspect of Termination – the Tenancy of Shops (Scotland) Acts 1949 and 1964

As we have seen, the purpose of this Act, when introduced, was to offer some comfort and protection to small shops facing inflated rents and other terms following the post-war era. It enabled tenants to apply to a sheriff for a renewal of their lease up to a year once they were in receipt of a notice to quit from the Landlord. The Act provides the tenant with a period of 21 days to make the application.

It would be fair to say, against this background, that I remain astonished that it was cited in both 2013 (*Edinburgh Woollen Mill Limited V Singh*) and 2015 (*Select Service Partner Limited V Network Rail*). In the first case, the Tenant's £161m turnover was a far cry from the predicament of the struggling shopkeepers immediately after the war. The second case in 2005 was also unsuccessful, albeit the court were at pains to emphasise that it was determined on the merits of the case.

It would be fair to say that this is, for me, the most obvious case for repeal of the 1949 and 1964 Acts as considered by the Discussion Paper. Indeed, it is the easiest of all the points considered in detail.

The Fifth Aspect of Termination – Irritancy

The Scots Law Commission are no strangers to proposing reform of irritancy, having done so originally in their Discussion Paper in 2001. The question being posed is whether there should be scope for a Landlord raising an action for damages arising from breach of contract for obligations preceding the date of irritancy. In my opinion, there is no great pressing need for this as, in practical terms, Landlords will either raise proceedings for breach of contract if the prospects of success are reasonable or, if not, proceed with irritancy in order to wipe the slate clean and start from scratch again. Most Landlords will also now consider rent deposit agreements and personal guarantees to comfort the blow of a defaulting Tenant during the term, especially where the covenant strength is not considered to be particularly strong at the outset.

The Sixth Aspect of Termination – Confusio and Consolidatio

As we have seen, *confusio* is where an obligation to do something comes to an end because debtor and creditor are one and the same. Similarly, *consolidatio* is where a subordinate real right – a right in the land of a 3rd party – is ended by virtue of the "*benefitted*" party subsequently acquiring ownership. Some academics have summarised that *consolidatio* generally applies to real rights whereas *confusio* applies to personal rights (but of course a registered long lease does create a real right in the property, so the original distinction appears to be a bit of a hybrid across both terms in the context of leases). It appears to be settled law that *confusio* takes place automatically whereas *consolidatio* does not but, historically, there is support in both camps on the question of whether, for example, confusion will terminate a servitude right where the benefitted proprietor subsequently becomes the heritable proprietor. Taking this a step further – and the main focus of the discussion paper in this regard – does *confusio* apply to a Lease where the Tenant subsequently acquires the heritable interest? The Keeper's present position in land registration applications is to accept confusion as applying unless it prejudices the position of a heritable creditor in a long leasehold title sheet. In my earlier chapters I made the point that the most recent House of Lords decision in *Clydesdale Bank Plc V Davidson* did not find a difficulty in suggesting *confusio* would apply where the same party holds the interest of both Landlord and Tenant.

The discussion paper explores instances and reasons where there may be a desire to keep the heritable and long leasehold title sheets alive. Scots law needs simplicity in this area and distinguishing tiers of interest in the same property by the same proprietor does not, in my view, rest well with that. If there was an instance where a Tenant wanted to keep an existing long leasehold interest alive in advance of its purchase then it is perfectly feasible for the lease to be assigned to another party – maybe a subsidiary, parent Co, or any other related party – so that the interest is clearly unaffected by the application of confusio. If there is a heritable creditor involved in the long leasehold interest then its interest could be protected by a necessity of obtaining consent before the leasehold interest is terminated once and for all. This would probably not be an issue if all sums were repaid under its facility and I would imagine any new lender funding the purchase would want this confirmed anyway. As we have seen earlier, the interest of a sub-tenant in such circumstances would not be prejudiced where Head Landlord and Mid-Landlord become the one and same. In the circumstances, I would welcome the law specifying that *confusio* would apply where Landlord and Tenant are the same entity but that the effective date would be the date of purchase where there is no security and the date of consent where there is a lender involved.

MORE BOOKS BY LAW BRIEF PUBLISHING

A selection of our other titles available now:-

'A Practical Guide to Solicitor and Client Costs – 2nd Edition' by Robin Dunne
'Constructive Dismissal – Practice Pointers and Principles' by Benjimin Burgher
'A Practical Guide to Religion and Belief Discrimination Claims in the Workplace' by Kashif Ali
'A Practical Guide to the Law of Medical Treatment Decisions' by Ben Troke
'Fundamental Dishonesty and QOCS in Personal Injury Proceedings: Law and Practice' by Jake Rowley
'A Practical Guide to the Law in Relation to School Exclusions' by Charlotte Hadfield & Alice de Coverley
'A Practical Guide to Divorce for the Silver Separators' by Karin Walker
'The Right to be Forgotten – The Law and Practical Issues' by Melissa Stock
'A Practical Guide to Planning Law and Rights of Way in National Parks, the Broads and AONBs' by James Maurici QC, James Neill et al
'A Practical Guide to Election Law' by Tom Tabori
'A Practical Guide to the Law in Relation to Surrogacy' by Andrew Powell
'A Practical Guide to Claims Arising from Fatal Accidents – 2nd Edition' by James Patience
'A Practical Guide to the Ownership of Employee Inventions – From Entitlement to Compensation' by James Tumbridge & Ashley Roughton
'A Practical Guide to Asbestos Claims' by Jonathan Owen & Gareth McAloon
'A Practical Guide to Stamp Duty Land Tax in England and Northern Ireland' by Suzanne O'Hara
'A Practical Guide to the Law of Farming Partnerships' by Philip Whitcomb

'Covid-19, Homeworking and the Law – The Essential Guide to Employment and GDPR Issues' by Forbes Solicitors

'Covid-19, Force Majeure and Frustration of Contracts – The Essential Guide' by Keith Markham

'Covid-19 and Criminal Law – The Essential Guide' by Ramya Nagesh

'Covid-19 and Family Law in England and Wales – The Essential Guide' by Safda Mahmood

'A Practical Guide to the Law of Unlawful Eviction and Harassment – 2nd Edition' by Stephanie Lovegrove

'Covid-19, Residential Property, Equity Release and Enfranchisement – The Essential Guide' by Paul Sams and Louise Uphill

'Covid-19, Brexit and the Law of Commercial Leases – The Essential Guide' by Mark Shelton

'A Practical Guide to Costs in Personal Injury Claims – 2nd Edition' by Matthew Hoe

'A Practical Guide to the General Data Protection Regulation (GDPR) – 2nd Edition' by Keith Markham

'Ellis on Credit Hire – Sixth Edition' by Aidan Ellis & Tim Kevan

'A Practical Guide to Working with Litigants in Person and McKenzie Friends in Family Cases' by Stuart Barlow

'Protecting Unregistered Brands: A Practical Guide to the Law of Passing Off' by Lorna Brazell

'A Practical Guide to Secondary Liability and Joint Enterprise Post-Jogee' by Joanne Cecil & James Mehigan

'A Practical Guide to the Pre-Action RTA Claims Protocol for Personal Injury Lawyers' by Antonia Ford

'A Practical Guide to Neighbour Disputes and the Law' by Alexander Walsh

'A Practical Guide to Forfeiture of Leases' by Mark Shelton

'A Practical Guide to Coercive Control for Legal Practitioners and Victims' by Rachel Horman

'A Practical Guide to Rights Over Airspace and Subsoil' by Daniel Gatty
'Tackling Disclosure in the Criminal Courts – A Practitioner's Guide' by Narita Bahra QC & Don Ramble
'A Practical Guide to the Law of Driverless Cars – Second Edition' by Alex Glassbrook, Emma Northey & Scarlett Milligan
'A Practical Guide to TOLATA Claims' by Greg Williams
'Artificial Intelligence – The Practical Legal Issues' by John Buyers
'A Practical Guide to the Law of Prescription in Scotland' by Andrew Foyle
'A Practical Guide to the Construction and Rectification of Wills and Trust Instruments' by Edward Hewitt
'A Practical Guide to the Law of Bullying and Harassment in the Workplace' by Philip Hyland
'How to Be a Freelance Solicitor: A Practical Guide to the SRA-Regulated Freelance Solicitor Model' by Paul Bennett
'A Practical Guide to Prison Injury Claims' by Malcolm Johnson
'A Practical Guide to the Small Claims Track' by Dominic Bright
'A Practical Guide to Advising Clients at the Police Station' by Colin Stephen McKeown-Beaumont
'A Practical Guide to Antisocial Behaviour Injunctions' by Iain Wightwick
'Practical Mediation: A Guide for Mediators, Advocates, Advisers, Lawyers, and Students in Civil, Commercial, Business, Property, Workplace, and Employment Cases' by Jonathan Dingle with John Sephton
'The Mini-Pupillage Workbook' by David Boyle
'A Practical Guide to Crofting Law' by Brian Inkster
'A Practical Guide to Spousal Maintenance' by Liz Cowell
'A Practical Guide to the Law of Domain Names and Cybersquatting' by Andrew Clemson
'A Practical Guide to the Law of Gender Pay Gap Reporting' by Harini Iyengar

'A Practical Guide to the Rights of Grandparents in Children Proceedings' by Stuart Barlow

'NHS Whistleblowing and the Law' by Joseph England

'Employment Law and the Gig Economy' by Nigel Mackay & Annie Powell

'A Practical Guide to Noise Induced Hearing Loss (NIHL) Claims' by Andrew Mckie, Ian Skeate, Gareth McAloon

'An Introduction to Beauty Negligence Claims – A Practical Guide for the Personal Injury Practitioner' by Greg Almond

'Intercompany Agreements for Transfer Pricing Compliance' by Paul Sutton

'Zen and the Art of Mediation' by Martin Plowman

'A Practical Guide to the SRA Principles, Individual and Law Firm Codes of Conduct 2019 – What Every Law Firm Needs to Know' by Paul Bennett

'A Practical Guide to Adoption for Family Lawyers' by Graham Pegg

'A Practical Guide to Industrial Disease Claims' by Andrew Mckie & Ian Skeate

'A Practical Guide to Redundancy' by Philip Hyland

'A Practical Guide to Vicarious Liability' by Mariel Irvine

'A Practical Guide to Applications for Landlord's Consent and Variation of Leases' by Mark Shelton

'A Practical Guide to Relief from Sanctions Post-Mitchell and Denton' by Peter Causton

'A Practical Guide to Equity Release for Advisors' by Paul Sams

'A Practical Guide to the Law Relating to Food' by Ian Thomas

'A Practical Guide to Financial Services Claims' by Chris Hegarty

'The Law of Houses in Multiple Occupation: A Practical Guide to HMO Proceedings' by Julian Hunt

'A Practical Guide to Unlawful Eviction and Harassment' by Stephanie Lovegrove

'Occupiers, Highways and Defective Premises Claims: A Practical Guide Post-Jackson – 2nd Edition' by Andrew Mckie

'A Practical Guide to Financial Ombudsman Service Claims' by Adam Temple & Robert Scrivenor
'A Practical Guide to Advising Schools on Employment Law' by Jonathan Holden
'A Practical Guide to Running Housing Disrepair and Cavity Wall Claims: 2nd Edition' by Andrew Mckie & Ian Skeate
'A Practical Guide to Holiday Sickness Claims – 2nd Edition' by Andrew Mckie & Ian Skeate
'Arguments and Tactics for Personal Injury and Clinical Negligence Claims' by Dorian Williams
'A Practical Guide to Drone Law' by Rufus Ballaster, Andrew Firman, Eleanor Clot
'A Practical Guide to Compliance for Personal Injury Firms Working With Claims Management Companies' by Paul Bennett
'A Practical Guide to Dog Law for Owners and Others' by Andrea Pitt
'RTA Allegations of Fraud in a Post-Jackson Era: The Handbook – 2nd Edition' by Andrew Mckie
'RTA Personal Injury Claims: A Practical Guide Post-Jackson' by Andrew Mckie
'On Experts: CPR35 for Lawyers and Experts' by David Boyle
'An Introduction to Personal Injury Law' by David Boyle
'A Practical Guide to Subtle Brain Injury Claims' by Pankaj Madan

www.ingramcontent.com/pod-product-compliance
Lightning Source LLC
LaVergne TN
LVHW022309200926
848481LV00004B/1256
* 9 7 8 1 9 1 3 7 1 5 3 0 4 *